ANOTHER COUNTRY

A Guide to the
Children's Books
of the
Lake District and Cumbria

by

James Mackenzie

Girls Gone By Publishers

Published by

Girls Gone By Publishers
4 Rock Terrace
Coleford
Bath
Somerset
BA3 5NF

First Edition
Published by Girls Gone By Publishers 2008
Text © James Mackenzie 2008
All uncredited photographs © James Mackenzie 2008
All other photographs © photographer as credited 2008
Sketch maps © James Mackenzie 2008
Design and Layout © Girls Gone By Publishers 2008
Cover photograph of Grasmere © Jenny Kisler 2008
Cover design © Girls Gone By Publishers 2008

Edited by Tig Thomas

Typeset in England by AJF
Printed in England by CPI Antony Rowe

ISBN 978-1-84745-048-7

Coniston from the south. The *Swallows and Amazons* Octopus Lagoon can be seen in the right foreground, and halfway up Coniston in the middle distance is Peel (Wild Cat) Island, very close to the High Peel Promontory (photographer: Peter Lewis).

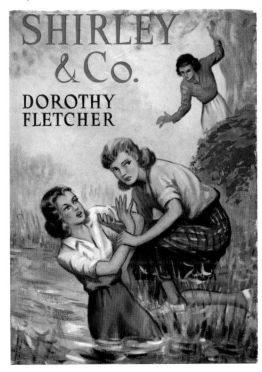

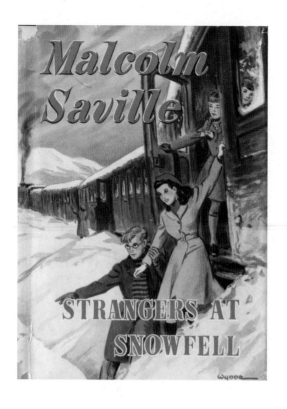

Malcolm Saville

STRANGERS AT SNOWFELL

The Hiding Place

Winifred Mantle

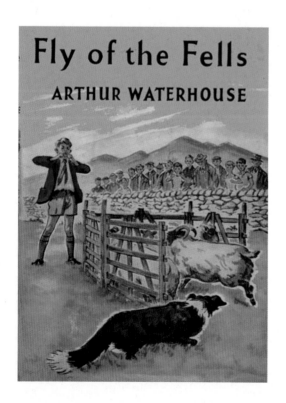

Fly of the Fells

ARTHUR WATERHOUSE

Falconsdale

Howard Jones

Blackie

FELL FARM
FOR
CHRISTMAS
Marjorie Lloyd

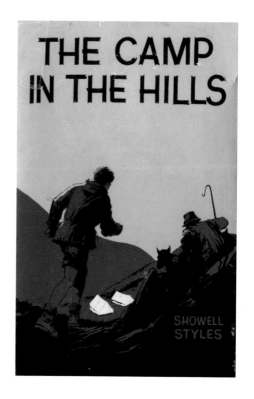

THE CAMP
IN THE HILLS
SHOWELL STYLES

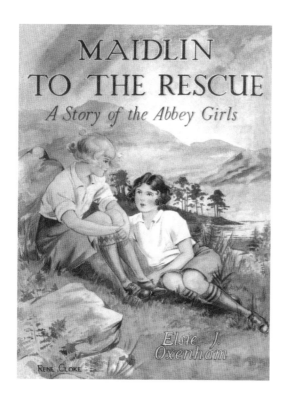

MAIDLIN
TO THE RESCUE
A Story of the Abbey Girls
Elsie J. Oxenham
RENE CLOKE

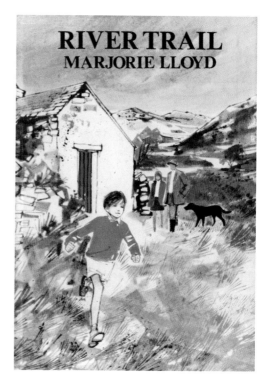

RIVER TRAIL
MARJORIE LLOYD

Sunset on the beach at St Bees (photographer: Tim Jolly)

Below left: Viking cross in Gosforth churchyard

Below right: Out on the La'al Ratty (photographer: Ruth Jolly)

Wast Water, the probable inspiration for Bannermere—'as blue as sapphire and as deep as sorrow' (photographer: Peter Lewis)

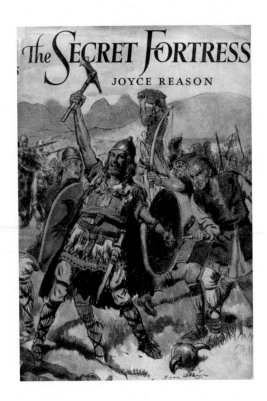

Damaris and Pip in *Damaris at Dorothy's*

Contents

List of colour illustrations

Front cover:
Grasmere, with elements from *Maidlin to the Rescue*; *Prefects at Vivians*; *Yan, the Story of a Lakeland Lamb*
Back cover
La'al Ratty

Colour pages:
Page 1
Top: Coniston from the south
Bottom: *No Boats on Bannermere*; *Shirley and Co.*

Page 2
Top: *Strangers at Snowfell*; *The Hiding Place*
Bottom: *Fly of the Fells*; *Falconsdale*

Page 3
Top: *Fell Farm for Christmas*; *The Camp in the Hills*
Bottom: *Maidlin to the Rescue*; *River Trail*

Page 4
Top: Sunset on the beach at St Bees
Bottom: Viking cross in Gosforth churchyard; Out on the La'al Ratty

Page 5
Top: Wast Water
Bottom: *The Gates of Bannerdale*; *The Secret Tarn*

Page 6
Top: The decorated boards of *In a Hand of Steel*; *The Secret Fortress*
Bottom: *Lakeland Adventure*; Damaris and Pip in *Damaris at Dorothy's*

To
ANGELA, JAMES AND PHILIP

INTRODUCTION

The train rattled on, the sea came into view on our left and the well-remembered shapes of the mountains on our right. The spring was later here, but there were daffodils already under the apple trees. The fells, crouched like great friendly dogs, still wore their last autumn coats of shaggy brown bracken, but very soon now the new green stalks would be pushing up and unfolding. The waterfalls were spuming down. When the train stopped at a little station, the gush and gurgle could sometimes be heard as a background to the voices on the platform.

We feasted our eyes on the scene we both loved.

THESE inspiring words by Geoffrey Trease come from *The Gates of Bannerdale* and tell of how Bill and Penny, the central characters in the Bannermere series, travel back to their home region of the Lake District after their first two terms at Oxford.

I invite you to come with me to make a similar journey to the landscapes that are loved by so many people. This guide can take you there to walk on the same ground, climb the same fells, gaze across the same lakes and even think the same thoughts as the many characters who appear in the 155 books which are explored in these pages.

On the other hand, your exciting journey may be purely imaginary. From the comfort of your own home you will find that some of the best children's writing of the last one hundred years is explored in these pages. Arthur Ransome, Geoffrey Trease, Rosemary Sutcliff, Elsie J Oxenham, John Rowe Townsend, Lorna Hill and Elfrida Vipont are just a handful of the famous names that will crop up as you get drawn into the extraordinary world of the lakes. You will meet both old favourites and many new treasures. The world of children's stories set in the Lake District really is bursting with extraordinary vitality and variety.

Where the story is easily available, I have kept the finer details of the plot largely untold and hope that you choose to read it yourself. However, where the book has gone out of print and few copies remain for sale on the second-hand market, I believe that the story deserves to be rescued through retelling.

Naturally, the countryside itself is a part of the magic. I have made the structure of the book a geographical one, with the different chapters following journeys round the various locations as I attempt to bring together each author's narrative with the places that inspired it. In the sections indicated by the boot symbol you will find my advice about how to visit the sites of crucial scenes in certain stories.

Finding Your Way through *Another Country*

Every book discussed within these pages has been assigned a number—see the book list on pages x–xiv. When the book is first discussed, it is identified by its number, which appears alongside in brackets.

The map on page xv breaks down the region into nine areas, as shown by the large grey numbers. These correspond to the chapter numbers. There is no number 10 on the map because Chapter X deals with those books that are difficult or impossible to pin down to one particular area.

Each chapter is headed by a more detailed map of the area it covers. The numbers on these maps represent the individual books from the book list, and have been placed nearest to each story's main location on the map. A number in italics indicates that my findings about the setting are only very speculative. A number underlined is used to show a setting, but also indicates that the major scenes from the story take place elsewhere and are usually depicted on other maps and discussed in another chapter. Single quotation marks around a fictional location suggest a reasonable guess about where the author intended a particular feature to be; eg 'Swallowdale'. Almost inevitably, certain books appear on more than one map; eg Julian Atterton's *Knights of the Lost Domain*, which has scenes in many different parts of Cumbria.

By referring to the map, the reader can at a glance place the book in its geographical context, and see how in many instances the lie of the land shaped the story. Of course, you can do things entirely the other way round—look at the map of a particular area, perhaps one you are visiting, then search the text to read about the books whose numbers appear on that map. By using Appendix II, you can start with a real location and trace easily which pages in this book will link you with the stories set in that place or nearby; or by using Appendix III, you can start instead with a book title.

The map of Bannermere in Chapter III and the map of Crummock Water and Buttermere which heads Chapter IX contain no numbers for reasons which become obvious during the course of the text.

Further Exploration

My maps are mere explanatory sketches, and for true exploration you can't do better than to consult the various Ordnance Survey Maps (Explorer Maps 004 to 007 for example) that together cover the whole area. Similarly, the walks or visits indicated by the boot symbol can only be enhanced by proper maps, specialist guide books and tourist board leaflets. More difficult walks, mentioned in passing in this book, should only be attempted after following the guidance given by local experts or by using a good map.

A Geographical Note

In 1974 the old counties of Cumberland and Westmorland, with part of the West Riding of Yorkshire and Lancashire 'north of the sands', were brought together under a local government body which was given the name of 'Cumbria'. Legally, this change did not affect the traditional counties or their boundaries; it simply imposed a new local authority structure. Indeed, societies have even been formed to preserve the old county names which nowadays have largely been forgotten by the media. Traditionalists will find that most of the children's books in this collection were written before 1974 and so retain the old names of the 'other' country to which I wish to lead you.

Book Titles

All book titles have been reproduced exactly as printed on their title page. This has sometimes led to seeming inconsistencies of style within this book, with, for example, full stops being used after 'Mr' and 'Mrs' in Beatrix Potter titles, but not when these words are used elsewhere within the text.

Inclusions, Omissions and Further Reading

You will look in vain in this manuscript for the myths, legends and folk-tales of Cumbria. Tempting as I found them, they fall outside the brief of this exploration. Cunningham's *Thorstein of the Mere*, with its boy living on Peel Island on Coniston, and perhaps inspiring Arthur Ransome's own children's stories, was not written with children in mind as the principal audience, so it too has been left out.

Nan Simpson's two stories *The Greenwood Elves* and *Bleaberry Village* were 'written in the woods surrounding Calder Abbey' but are merely an invitation for the reader to create 'their own Elfland'. Reluctantly, one must yield to the idea that, although inspired by the Cumbrian landscape, they are tales that belong to the special and indeterminate world of the author's, and the child reader's, imagination.

Beatrix Potter and the inspiration she gained from her holidays near Derwentwater and her home at Sawrey fill a comparatively short space in these pages. Her remarkable life and the Lakeland adventures of her characters have been covered in more detail in many other books.

The chapter on Arthur Ransome in this book offers a very personal view of his Lakeland, in addition to the many other resources available for this author. The splendid books by Christina Hardyment, Clare Kendall-Price and Roger Wardale will take you further into his world than you might think possible.

Finally, I do not claim to have discovered all the children's stories of the Lake District and would be delighted to learn the titles of any more. Let us hope that this journey we can take together may never end. For I have found that the Lake District is undoubtedly a magical setting for children's stories and a captivating place to go and visit. I hope that you too, after reading these pages, will share my belief that there is indeed 'another country' out there for you to discover and to share with your friends and your children.

James Mackenzie
2008

THE BOOKS TO BE FOUND IN
ANOTHER COUNTRY

CUMBRIA AND NORTH LANCASHIRE

WITH CHAPTER NUMBERS

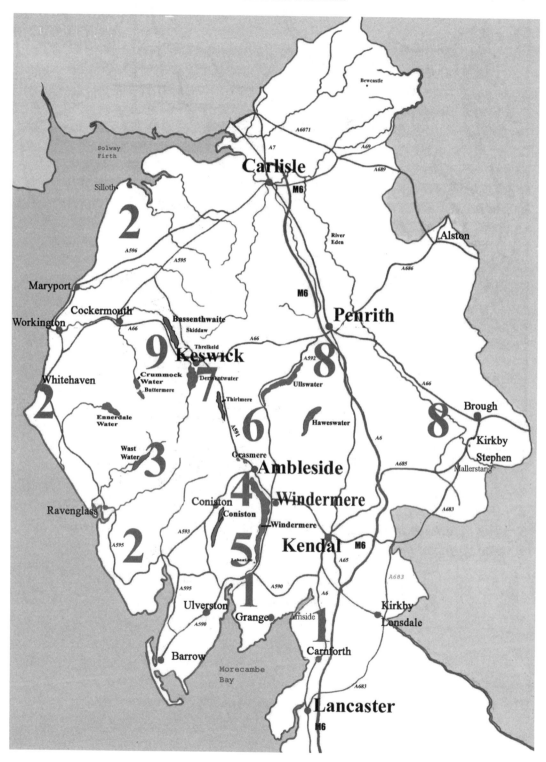

MORECAMBE BAY

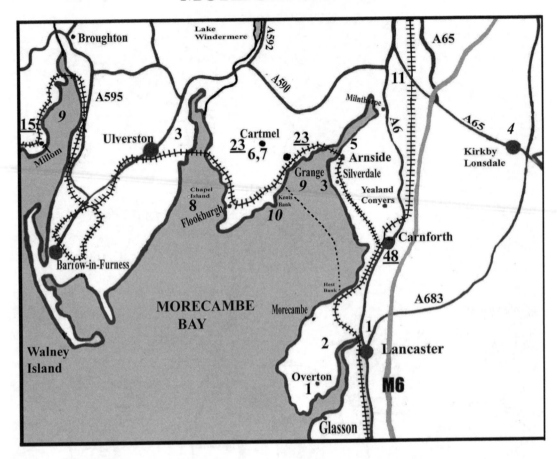

CHAPTER I

THE SEA, THE RIVERS AND THE SHIFTING SANDS

Morecambe Bay, Lancaster, Arnside, Kirkby Lonsdale,
Grange-Over-Sands, Cartmel, Ulverston

IMAGINE that the large area of grey that covers most of the map opposite is the sea. Now imagine that for much of the time that same colour is the yellow and brown of sand and mud. For Morecambe Bay is the second largest bay in the United Kingdom—only the Wash is bigger. Stretching from Walney Island in the north to Fleetwood in the south, it is the largest continuous inter-tidal area in the whole of Britain. The Bay is both broad and shallow and the tide rushes in to the shore at the speed of a galloping horse. An area the size of a football pitch can be covered in a few minutes. Several rivers flow into the bay, including the Kent, Leven, Lune and Duddon. Between the rivers lie the lands of the southern Lake District peninsulas and the north-west Lancashire coast. A dotted line from Kent's Bank to Hest Bank shows that with the special Queen's Sand Guide in attendance, and with your heart in your mouth, it is just possible to walk from one shore to the other. The books in this chapter will soon make you realise that you must never venture out alone!

Jacobites and Smugglers—Lancaster and Morecambe Bay

Our exploration of the North Lancashire and Morecambe Bay section of this region through its children's books actually begins on the Isle of Man. It also begins back in the troubled eighteenth century, where the apparently sleepy countryside was a hotbed of crime and espionage. Stories of smugglers in Cornwall and the south west are a well-known theme of children's literature. Less has been written about the doings of the men of the mud flats of the north Lancashire coast.

As we shall see in *Lanterns over the Lune* (1) by Kathleen Fidler, published in 1958, nowhere could be better for a halfway house for such illegal activities than amongst the unscrupulous traders on the isle of the Manxmen.

Simon Corlett is the name of the young hero, and he is almost fifteen at the beginning of the story. After the death of his father, Simon makes up his mind to run away from the Isle of Man and head, if possible, for Lancashire, which is where his mother came from. He stows away on one of the smugglers' ships making for the Lune Estuary, which leads to the ancient city of Lancaster. To his horror, in the darkness of the night Simon overhears the captain, a disgusting rogue called Skillicorn, plan the turning over of a Jacobite agent to the government forces. Both Simon and the agent must escape. There is no way out but to leap into the pitchy-black water and clamber on to the mud near the small villages of Overton and Glasson. Their enemies soon come

Sunderland Point: the first sight of Bridget's
home (illustration by David Walsh)

after them 'into the waist-deep icy water, cursing and swearing as they [gasp] with the cold'.

The pursuit is relentless and Simon finally staggers into the shelter of some undergrowth, clutching the secret packet that the agent has thrust into his hands. Within seconds he hears Skillicorn gloat as the shots ring out and the crew strip the dead body of the unlucky Jacobite. Simon knows that the vicious smugglers will still be after him to recover the documents he carries. He stumbles on across the marshes. Back into the river he must go and take his chance on the other side of the treacherous Lune.

His luck finally changes when he makes it to the house of Joshua Lawson at Sunderland Point. Here he finds kindness and a haven of rest before being plunged into the next stage of his nightmare. He also meets young Bridget Lawson, the niece of a rich merchant, whose sympathies at this time lie with the Jacobites. At first it seems that Bridget considers Simon to be beneath her notice. However, in a crucial incident he risks his life to save her gown from the mud, and almost at once she begins to respect him.

Nevertheless, the Jacobite cause hasn't finished with either of them yet. The 1715 Jacobite rebellion is under way, and the reader learns of how the rebels are moving gradually from Kirkby Lonsdale to Lancaster. Whilst searching for his family roots near Lancaster, Simon finds himself marched away to rebellion, only to see the entire Jacobite army surrounded in Preston and then tamely surrender. Both Simon and Bridget have many more dangers to face, including a ferocious encounter with the ruthless smugglers, before he can make his escape back down the river to a new life in the Colonies. His last thoughts are of Bridget and her safety. He will surely return.

The sight of the lantern she displays reassures him that she is in her room, and we now learn that the 'lanterns' of the title are not just a symbol of smuggling going on on the river, but a sign of the bond of trust that has grown between the two young people.

Then the sails were raised and down the shining river the *Robert* sailed, a silver ship on a silver tide, bound for the New World. Across the water the light of a lantern set in a window shone steadily. Simon watched it until the ship bore him away.

The lower Lune Estuary and the historic port of Glasson Dock are still accessible today. The best place to head for is the Conder Green picnic site near the end of the Lune Millennium Cycleway. The site is four miles to the south of Lancaster, just off the A588, and is half a mile from Glasson. The path starts near Glasson Dock and follows a disused railway line alongside the river. It can be followed all the way into Aldcliffe and then on into Lancaster itself.

Before we leave the southernmost point of our literary region, another book, *The School Library Mystery* (2) by Agnes Furlong, published in 1951, draws our attention again to the ancient county town of Lancaster.

Agnes Furlong calls the setting of her mystery story 'Lonchester' and refers constantly to the 'River Lon', but it does not require the deductive abilities of a Sherlock Holmes to work out that she is thinking of Lancaster and the River Lune. Once again, as with *Lanterns over the Lune*, the story concerns itself with the Jacobites and the effect that their incursions into England in the cause of the Stuart monarchy had upon this particular region. However, the story is set contemporarily with the period in which it was written, ie the 1950s, and concerns the investigations carried out into the 1745 rebellion by a group of fifteen-year-olds at a co-educational grammar school in the town.

In the library, June discovers a mysterious paper in the lining of an old edition of Daniel Defoe's *Tour through the Whole Island of Great Britain*. On it is a rhyme that leads them back into the events of 1745 and the people who were living at that time. Unfortunately, an opportunist thief secures the paper and the four young people soon find themselves working against a deadly rival.

From this point onwards, Agnes Furlong makes full use of the potential of various settings in Lancaster but principally the famous castle, the remains of the church on the same hill and the old houses and warehouses to be found on the quayside.

The events of the rebellion, the past trading history of Lancaster, the selection of ancient buildings of the town, are all woven together into an interesting and well-paced narrative.

The City of Lancaster is dominated by its medieval castle, but also by the River Lune, which runs through its centre. It was originally a Roman settlement—Lun Castrum—the fort on the River Lune. Today you can still walk the narrow Georgian streets, climb Castle Hill to the famous Priory Church and explore the City Museum in the Market Square and the Maritime Museum on the quayside. After having read the book, you will see that it is perfectly possible to stand in the right places and imagine exactly what the young people did. In particular, you could find yourself wondering if there really is a hidden passage where the author suggests it.

If you take the A6 out of Lancaster, you soon come to the turning for the little village of Yealand Conyers. The notable children's author Elfrida Vipont was born in Manchester in 1902, but moved to Yealand Conyers during the Second World War to run a school for evacuated Quaker children at Yealand Manor. *The Heir of Craigs* (3), published in 1955, which she wrote under the pseudonym of Charles Vipont, is a book which draws upon all her experience of the sands of Morecambe Bay, which were adjacent to her home. The fictional Craigs itself proves to be a grim old mansion built on the most desolate part of the coast not far from Silverdale, then a fishing village with easy access to the sea.

Once again Jacobite intrigue lurks in the background of the life of Nigel, the eponymous young heir. But the horror in this story comes from both his wicked Uncle Askew and the malign clutch of the sinking sands that surround him.

It has a truly chilling opening. Playing truant from his lessons one day, Nigel witnesses with growing apprehension the arrival of a stranger who approaches across the sands.

> Soon, if he continued on his way, the sands would swallow him up. His horse would thresh helplessly in the mire, with long neck tossing and eyes rolling in terror, and he would leap for safety, only to be engulfed the faster.

It is only the admiration he feels for the horse that prompts Nigel into giving the necessary warning. It turns out that the stranger is his older cousin Nicholas, who has come to enlist support for the Jacobite claimant. In a cynical response, Uncle Askew sends the young man on his way to cross the Kent Estuary at a tide time that he knows is too late for safety. Once again, Nigel has to save his cousin, and he loses his own horse as they struggle back to shore. Later, on another more inspiring journey to the Kent's Bank shore, they encounter the remarkable Mistress Fox of Swarthmore Hall, a leading Quaker who has come through the ordeal of imprisonment sustained by her beliefs.

Back in the appalling house of Craigs, the two cousins are forced to flee when they finally realise that Uncle Askew is determined to seize some recovered family jewels and then take their lives. They complete a desperate escape by being rowed out to a sailing vessel near Silverdale. Nicholas has made up his mind to sail to the New World, and the long central portion of the book concerns the dreadful adventures which the two cousins are forced to survive before they return to Europe. Here a visit to the exiled King James's court at St Germain convinces Nicholas that their future must lie over the Atlantic once more in America, but first they are drawn back to Craigs. They land at Plumpton near Ulverston and, filled with foreboding, wait for the tide so they can cross Leven Sands for their final encounter with Askew at the creepy mansion.

A tragedy remains to be played out at Craigs on the sands of Morecambe Bay, but it is Elfrida Vipont's job to bring you the actual details. Like the rest of her book, it is well worth reading.

 You too may visit the home of Mistress Fox. The Society of Friends, or Quakers, advertise on their website that Swarthmoor Hall in Ulverston, one of the earliest headquarters of their movement, is open to the public for a guided tour from mid-March until mid-October on a Thursday, Saturday, and Sunday at 2.30 pm and at other times when staff are free.

A Diversion to Kirkby Lonsdale

Part of Elfrida Vipont's story has already led us on further round the coast of Morecambe Bay, but before we follow further the road or indeed the railway round the fringes of the sea and the infamous sands, it is sensible to use the map to nip in and out of the county of nearby Yorkshire to the east. This takes us on the A683 north from Lancaster to Kirkby Lonsdale and to the book called **Wayland's Keep** (4) by Angela Bull, published in 1966.

This is a very cleverly constructed and well-written story about two groups of children living in different centuries. Without resorting to fantasies or time-slip devices, Angela Bull brings together the members of the Egerton family of the late nineteenth century and the cousins Malinda, Sophie and Anna in the 1960s.

Sisters Sophie and Anna begin by thoroughly disliking and being slightly in awe of their cousin Malinda, a very intelligent and seemingly worldly-wise twelve-year-old. Malinda, chic and self-contained, appears to despise her cousins for their lack of penetration and assertiveness. However, a family mystery brings them together, and as they assemble the facts about Wayland and his loving sister Emily, each realises that the others have a lot to offer. In the end it is Anna who thinks her way through to the truth and reveals the tragedy at the heart of the mystery. All three girls have grown through their co-operation and resolve to turn what they have learned into a book, taking equal shares in both the endeavour itself and the credit that may follow.

The book is set on the edges of Westmorland with the real mountains just a distant prospect. The author's biographical details give the best clue to the places that may have inspired her creation. She taught for a year at Casterton School in the village of the same name. The journey from there to nearby Kirkby Lonsdale may have been the inspiration for the trips made by both the modern and Victorian children to the small market town she calls Burstall.

A quick glance at the history of the school traces it back to its origins in Cowan Bridge, and it proves to be the school to which the Brontë sisters went in 1824–25, and which emerged later in *Jane Eyre* as 'Lowood'. But that's another story.

The First Taste of the Lakes—Arnside

Let us now return to the coast and turn the corner in order to make the dangerous crossing of the Kent Estuary. We also move for a while from the books which could be classed as junior historical novels to those that can be regarded as family adventure stories.

The Beresford family: Roger in the doorway, John in the corner, Pat nearest the reader and Dinah with her foot near the rope (illustration by Geoffrey Day)

There are three books concerning the Beresford children, John, Pat, Roger and Dinah, whose home is somewhere near an elusive lake in central Lakeland, the precise location of which I consider in Chapter V, pages 74–76. In his 1954 book, *The Beresfords in Tarndale* (5), which is their final Lakeland adventure, Peter Lethbridge uses a whole series of fictional names to disguise the setting of the place where they are on holiday. This gives him the leeway to adapt the countryside to exactly the adventure he wants to create. There are several river estuaries at the foot of the Lake District that could be the model for Tarndale, but the Kent Estuary and Arnside appear to offer the best match to so many of the locations that appear in the narrative. A quick survey of its features would include the sleepy little town, the estuary, which is aligned north-south, the railway on stone piers that crosses the water, the hill above (Arnside Knott) from which the panoramic view is obtained, the ruined peel tower on Tower Farm and the occurrence nearby of the limestone pavements that support the growth of a profusion of lilies-of-the-valley—all these can be ticked on the list. Perhaps the 'arn' in Tarndale is also meant to be a sly indication of Arnside.

The plot of this final Beresford Lake District story has a strange charm of its own. It must be one of the few children's mysteries which has flower stealing as the main activity of the villains! Once again the thieves in the story come from the sea, crossing the bay from those nearby centres of trouble, Morecambe and Blackpool.

Arnside, the possible Tarndale, is another of those locations that you can visit yourself. By road or by rail you can reach the little sea-front parade of shops and pubs and gaze out over the extraordinary Kent Estuary. As you stand there you can remember that this is where Arthur Ransome's famous *Swallow* was built, and this is where you can first begin to drink in the distant prospect of the southern fells and imagine the lakes where the famous little dinghy went on her great adventures. As the train creaks across the stunning fifty piers of the viaduct, perhaps you will also hear the strident horn which is blown to frighten you off the sands before the sea and the mud can claim you. More pleasantly, you can certainly and safely take the walk to Arnside Knott and look down over the town, the river and the bridge, just as the Beresfords do in the story. The footpath is well signposted, and there is also similar clear guidance to the ruined peel tower which features so prominently early in their adventure. A peel tower, a feature of this area, was a fortified house or dwelling place, normally entered by ladder to the first floor, with a vaulted ground floor for the cattle. They are usually found on the borderlands of England and Scotland.

After it crosses the long and picturesque viaduct, the railway goes on to the rather prim and subdued Edwardian seaside resort of Grange-Over-Sands with its beautifully renovated station, its long quiet promenade, its ornamental gardens and its interesting shops. The only children's story with a scene set in this charming town is *Left until*

The old Arnside viaduct crossing the Kent estuary, now replaced by stone piers

Above: Arnside with Arnside Knott behind (photographer: Bill Hunter)
Below: The splendidly restored station at Grange-Over-Sands

Called for at Vivians **(23)** (see page 27), which is described in detail in Chapter II of this book. However, the journey through Hampsfell behind the upper houses of the seaside town is one that must not be neglected. On the other side of the hill is a treasure to be found.

The Unexpected Treasure

Amongst my last discoveries before this book was completed were the two stories by Elfrida Vipont that tell the story of Laura Haverard. Her 1957 book *The Spring of the Year* **(6)**, and *Flowering Spring* **(7)**, published in 1960, are mostly set in a location that is obvious once you see the clues. The credit must go to the critic Marcus Crouch, who, in *The Nesbit Tradition*, identified St Merlyon as Cartmel; for one short visit to the place at the foot of Hampsfell is all you will need to confirm that he was right. Vipont draws once again upon her Quaker background to create a career story which echoes that of her heroine in the Carnegie Medal-winning *The Lark on the Wing*.

Professor Haverard uproots his family from Oxford to help found a new university in the north of England, and whilst on a preliminary visit to the area, by a happy accident sees a signpost for St Merlyon. Because it mentions an old priory, his youngest daughter, Laura, persuades her father to go and have a look at it.

> St Merlyon was a big village with cobbled streets and a cobbled square with a preaching cross in the middle of it. A broad, shallow stream ran through it, and you could lean over the old stone bridge and watch the fish darting to and fro, and hiding in the swaying water-weeds on the pebbly bottom.

Very soon they discover the Priory church: 'The Priory was a very old church, and when you pushed through the heavy doorway you felt swallowed up in the silence.'

As each of the family looks around the village, they come to the conclusion that somehow 'it all belongs', an image for them that everything is in harmony. The presence of a small Quaker meeting house, most probably based on the one in Yealand Conyers, confirms this feeling. By the end of the book, the reader has been introduced to many details that can still be recognised in the Cartmel of fifty years later.

Nowadays, after parking in the generous-sized parking area allocated to the racecourse, you can easily walk around the unpretentious market square, gaze into secluded corners filled with flowers, and visit specialist shops for books, crafts and food. Best of all, there is the church with the odd towers which was once part of Cartmel Priory, one of the finest and most atmospheric religious buildings of northern Britain. Wandering the quiet lanes, traversing the almost unnoticed bridges and investigating the nearby footpath, it is not surprising to find yourself thinking of the legend that the twelfth-century Priory was built between two parallel streams in response to a 'Heavenly Voice'. Whilst there, you also can reach out for the magic that Vipont created for the Haverard family.

On Laura's first visit the compulsion to stay forever comes drifting into her life via the water at the end of the garden.

> Suddenly a paper boat came sailing downstream. It was a well-made craft, and it carried a cargo of three chocolate beans, yellow and brown and red.
> She reached out to pull it ashore. As she did so, she saw a girl of about her own age, pink-cheeked, with red-gold hair and blue eyes, standing in the next garden.
> 'When you come and live here, can you and I be friends?' asked Katie.

The story is indeed partly about a special friendship, but it is not long before we realise just how completely these two books belong to the longer sequence of stories about the Haverard family that began with *The Lark in the Morn*. They are not simply about the trials faced by any young girls growing up, but about how the gifted interpretative artists of this world have to develop in character in order to be a success in their chosen art. With Kit Haverard in *The Lark on the Wing*, her plans for a career in music are opposed by her effective but basically insensitive guardian. The theme that emerges is, of course, the age-old one of 'being true to yourself' in order to succeed. After her Carnegie Medal success, Elfrida Vipont returned to the same idea in her St Merlyon/Cartmel stories, but looked at it from an entirely different viewpoint.

This time Laura's long road to success and fulfilment consists of learning what her real self is. Only then can she move forward as an actress. Ironically, Laura has to grow in self-knowledge at the same time as she has to stop thinking about the impression she is making. At the beginning of *The Spring of the Year* she is suffering from

Through the Cartmel Priory gatehouse arch to the Market Cross

being the odd one out in her family; Mary is clever, the twins are pretty and personable, and Christopher is a boy. Laura has a tendency to see the world ranged against her and to complain of unfairness. When the primary school teacher gives her the part of Mary in the Christmas play over the head of her new friend Katie, to whom the part should have gone by tradition, she is at first too self-centred to do the right thing and refuse it. The nativity play incident is balanced by one at the end of *Flowering Spring*, when her part of Juliet in a village production is arbitrarily given away by the star-struck producer to her famous actress cousin, Millie, who has taken a whim to appear in it. When Millie inevitably lets the producer down, Laura's pride at first refuses to let her have anything more to do with the play. It is her hard-learnt knowledge that one must not allow personal feelings ever to get in the way of the part that leads her to take it and to make a supreme success of it.

A vital part of the triumph of the first book is the way in which Vipont explores a personal and family crisis against the plausible background of the social and educational realities of her carefully created small community. That she, a professor's child, should fail to get into grammar school is a tremendous challenge to Laura's self-esteem. However, her decision to refuse the offer of boarding school, and to take up her place at a local secondary modern, where she can be more herself, is one of her early steps to that essential self-knowledge. More satisfyingly, the reader discovers that Laura is not the only one with a lesson to learn. Laura's father, a rigid academic with little sympathy for his children, is made to realise that it is no good forcing people into roles that aren't right for them. Even Laura's kindly, easy-going mother has to acknowledge that she shouldn't try to live out her dreams through her children when the lively twins hijack a village entertainment by crooning popular songs and jiving in scarlet sweaters instead of performing the decorous classical music their mother had intended.

It is with these small yet important episodes of village life that the author develops the strong sense of family and of place. At the centre of both stories is the Priory, whose fortunes are woven in with Laura's, and which stands for the integrity and permanence of St Merlyon. In *The Spring of the Year* it is the Priory festival that draws the village together and offers one of Laura's earliest successes at acting; in *Flowering Spring* a valuable prayer book stolen from the Priory, partly due to Laura's love of an audience, provides a tense but compassionate subplot.

Without doubt the discerning reader can find a great deal of fulfilment in watching this rather unpromising heroine pass through some crucial stages in her life in a place which comes to have both a specific and a universal appeal. By the end of the first book each member of the Haverard family has realised the truth of the words the Rector quoted when he first met them:

'So he bringeth them unto the haven where they would be.'

They are now a part of that strange feeling of belonging.

Be assured that the quiet stream, the winding streets, the old-fashioned houses, the

Priory gatehouse, and the Priory church with its strange towers, are still all there to be discovered, in the small town of Cartmel or in the pages of these two uplifting and engaging stories.

A Tidal Race to Chapel Island

Once again, the scene switches suddenly back to the coast.

The central episodes of *The Mystery Prize* (8), by Helen Kent, are, as we shall see, set around the shores of Lake Windermere. However, during the summer holidays the heroine, Hope Harland, unable to return to her own home because of her grandmother's illness, spends part of her time with Mrs Lodore, guardian to young Garth. Mrs Lodore lives at her bungalow on the sands at Sandycrest on Morecambe Bay. From a consideration of the clues within the text, this would appear to be on the coast near Flookburgh.

One day a complex set of circumstances arises which means that Hope is left alone at Sandycrest with the inexperienced nurse, Ann, in charge of Garth. While Hope writes some letters and then practises assiduously at the piano, the day slowly but surely begins to develop tragic possibilities.

> Suddenly it occurred to Hope that, now her own music had ceased, all was unusually silent and still, save for a far-off moaning sound, too low and indistinct for the girl to realise at first what it was.

Slowly Hope begins to comprehend what is happening without fully realising the awful horror that is about to unfold.

> The weather was changing rapidly, bringing with it a cool breeze from across the sea. The clouds were rising higher every second, threatening a coming storm of rain. Far away, a long white line marked the wave-crests of the open sea. The tide had turned, and the water was advancing quickly across the sands, with the storm in the rear.

The cook's question about the whereabouts of Ann and young Garth brings the truth home with stunning force. The inexperienced Ann is wheeling young Garth across the open sands of the Leven Estuary whilst reading a novelette and is oblivious to the danger that is overtaking them!

In spite of a recent debilitating illness, Hope sets off across the sands to the tiny figures in the distance. By the time she reaches the errant maid, Hope's heart is almost at bursting point.

> 'Ann! The tide! Look!'
> Ann did look—and then she screamed aloud. No wonder! There, advancing up the river estuary, and spreading across the sands with

inconceivable speed, was the ominous tawny line of yellow foam, followed by racing waves that had behind them the force of an oncoming gale.

Rescue on the sands

The author then gives this scene of horrified panic an exact location. They are close to Chapel Island in the Leven Estuary. The island indeed proves a place of refuge for young Garth, the silly Ann and the worthy Hope. That people still seek safety on this scrap of land is confirmed by an inspection of the recent 'shouts' of the local lifeboat service as recorded on the internet.

As I have said, the larger picture of Hope's life is completed at the school near Lake Windermere, and this flight across the sands is no more than an episode in her story, which is examined in detail in Chapter V, page 71. For a more unrelenting picture of life on the edge of the treacherous estuaries, we must turn elsewhere.

A Coastal Nightmare

The Intruder (9) by John Rowe Townsend, published in 1969, is a book about suffering, and at times it generates an extraordinary feeling of oppression. This partly arises from the author's marvellous, almost poetic evocation of the setting, and partly from the skilful way in which he develops the form of nightmare that gradually starts to overwhelm sixteen-year-old Arnold Haithwaite.

One is forced to assume that the setting is a conglomerate one, assembled from many of the different elements that go towards the make-up of both the southern and western coasts of Furness and Cumbria. He gives his dilapidated silted-up coastal village the name of Skirl and then reduces the essence of the place to the same five-word phrase that both begins and ends the book:

Sea, sand, stone, slate, sky.

There are clues to the real places that inspired Townsend's creation of Skirl, but they are mixed with half-clues that can easily set you on the wrong track. The Ellisons, the incoming family in the book, have a father who works as an engineer building the nuclear power station, known by the locals as 'The Atomic', just five miles up the coast. The estuary of the Skirl leads not on to Morecambe Bay but on to the Irish Sea. The sketch map that accompanies the book suggests high fells immediately to the east. Thus Skirl could be said to be based upon the geographical position of Ravenglass, with Sellafield about the right distance away. However, the job of a sand pilot, a feature

You have been warned!

of the book, is only nowadays associated with the walk from Hest Bank to near Grange, which makes the nuclear power stations at Heysham a possibility.

There are many convincing character portrayals in this book, but none can rival that of Sonny, the outsider who manages to insinuate himself into the small community and even into Arnold's home. Just as the shifting sands can suck the life out of the unwary traveller, so both young Arnold and the old man whom he believes to be his grandfather are drained of the will to resist him. Sonny's claim to be the real Arnold Haithwaite undermines all the vulnerable boy's roots in the community, for he knows there is a mystery surrounding his parentage. Towards the end of the book Sonny's attack on the cotton tree is a symbolic confirmation that he is a force bent on destruction. Ironically this assault on the two hundred-year-old tree also ensures his own ultimate failure—it is the one thing that rouses the Duchy of Lancaster's agent into immediate action and it provokes the dramatic climax in the middle of one of the worst storms ever to strike Skirl. The sixteen-year-old Arnold finds himself, during the course of one wild night, to be both the preserver of life and the cause of death.

Nowhere will you find a better description of the sheer horror of being trapped out on the sands as the waves and the tide come tearing in. The sea is the enemy; and even when faced with the appalling intruder who has driven him out of his home, Arnold still recognises the responsibility he carries, which asserts that he must try to preserve all life, no matter how detestable. This is an extraordinarily gripping book, for, without ever resorting to fantasy, it introduces the reader to a period of sustained and almost claustrophobic horror.

Into the Mud

A similar vagueness of location applies to the short story 'Where None Has Walked Before' by Arthur Catherall, the Bolton-born writer of hundreds of stories for both boys and girls. The story in question comes from *Adventurers, Ltd.* **(10)**, a collection of tales published in 1954, about the doings of a particular Boy Scout patrol. One of the estuaries of Morecambe Bay is renamed Duckeram Bay, and the boys are cycling on their way at the edge of the sands, hoping to spend a quiet weekend studying the seabirds and waders that gather there in profusion. Andy Sprigg, in charge, leads all the others into a near collision with a group of sheep which had gathered by the narrow roadside. Two of the beasts, thoroughly spooked, lumber frantically on to the sands. 'They had run straight out, as if intent on crossing the thousand yard wide estuary, but after some forty yards they had slowed down, and now they were stopped and bleating helplessly.' It is soon clear they are trapped in the mud and doomed to drown. Andy decides to make one more attempt at saving the wretched animals by fixing the wooden boards from a broken orange box to his feet and using them as skis to cross the mud. He fails miserably.

The turning point of the story comes with the discovery of an unknown man and the 'splatchers' that they find attached to his feet. It is perhaps appropriate that a device used so effectively in Arthur Ransome's *Secret Water* on the Essex coast should find its usage replicated here on a coast well known to the famous author.

'The River Comes First'

It is worth ending this stage of our exploration by taking a tentative step north into Ransome territory, in order to mention those stories about this section of his world not so well known to the fans of the Swallows and Amazons series. In his interesting collection *Coots in the North & Other Stories* **(11)**, published in 1988, Hugh Brogan brought together for the first time some of the scraps of Ransome's writing that had never previously been published for a wide audience. These included two extracts of a longer story that was to be called 'The River Comes First'.

The river in question is the Bela, which flows into the Kent Estuary at Sandside and which in its upstream stretches is known as the Stainton Beck, from the village of Stainton through which it runs. For Arthur Ransome, the devoted angler, the Bela was one of the main reasons for living in Cumbria, and the family connections with the Bela fishing association and its river warden went back to his grandfather's days.

Some of the extracts were written in the customary third person that marks out the Swallows and Amazons stories, but as he struggled to find the right voice for the story, there was also a significant section called 'The Cloudburst', in which the first person narrative gives a sense of immediacy that it is hard to match anywhere else in his writing. Those who buy Hugh Brogan's *Coots in the North* volume in pursuit of the elusive, unfinished thirteenth Swallows and Amazons adventure will be amply rewarded by the two extracts about a boy and this little river of the southern peninsulas.

THE WEST COAST

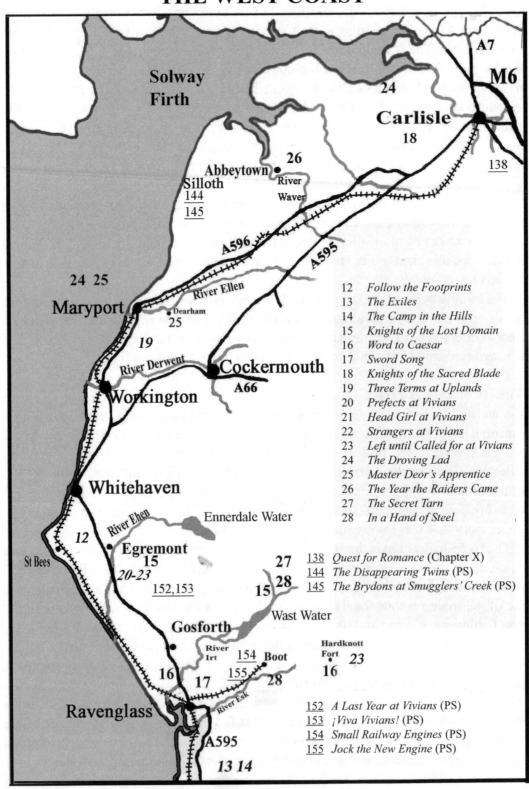

Solway Firth

A7

M6

24

Carlisle
18

138

26

Abbeytown
River Waver

Silloth
144
145

A596

A595

24 25

River Ellen

Maryport

Dearham
25

19

River Derwent

Cockermouth
A66

Workington

12   Follow the Footprints
13   The Exiles
14   The Camp in the Hills
15   Knights of the Lost Domain
16   Word to Caesar
17   Sword Song
18   Knights of the Sacred Blade
19   Three Terms at Uplands
20   Prefects at Vivians
21   Head Girl at Vivians
22   Strangers at Vivians
23   Left until Called for at Vivians
24   The Droving Lad
25   Master Deor's Apprentice
26   The Year the Raiders Came
27   The Secret Tarn
28   In a Hand of Steel

Whitehaven

River Ehen

Ennerdale Water

St Bees

12

Egremont
15
20-23

152,153

27

28

15

138   Quest for Romance (Chapter X)
144   The Disappearing Twins (PS)
145   The Brydons at Smugglers' Creek (PS)

Wast Water

Gosforth

River Irt

154   Boot

Hardknott Fort   23

16

155

28

16   17

River Esk

Ravenglass

A595

13 14

152   A Last Year at Vivians (PS)
153   ¡Viva Vivians! (PS)
154   Small Railway Engines (PS)
155   Jock the New Engine (PS)

CHAPTER II

OUT ON THE COAST AND UP INTO
THE HILLS

Millom, Ravenglass, Maryport, Solway Firth, Eskdale, Wasdale, Carlisle

As we continue to travel round the outer rim of the Lake District, it soon becomes clear that the long and varied coastline between Morecambe Bay and the Solway Firth offers a series of dramatic contrasts. In the south, there is a narrow corridor between the mountains and the Irish Sea that is threaded by the West Coast Railway and the A595. Here you encounter sand dunes and salt marshes at Ravenglass and then find the tremendous sandstone cliffs at St Bees. Move further north through the industrial belt of Sellafield, Workington and Whitehaven, and you will come across the extensive farmlands of the Solway Plain. This is a gentler countryside with a charm all of its own as the rivers Wampool and Waver wander placidly towards the sea. Yet just to the east lie the tremendous valleys of Eskdale, Wasdale and Ennerdale and the brooding heights that surround them.

Let us begin our exploration of the western coast of Cumbria by a consideration of three books which, without pinning themselves down to any particular identifiable locations, make free use of the general characteristics of the lands between the mountains and the Irish Sea.

The Mysterious Abbey
Even the most casual search on the internet for ruined religious houses in Cumbria will bring up the names of at least four abbeys and several priories. Thus when William Mayne, Carnegie Medal winner and expert on the Yorkshire Dales, wrote his first book, *Follow the Footprints* (12), published in 1953, and set it near an abbey in Cumberland, there were many real places that sprang into contention to be the actual abbey. However, once again it is the old story of a writer identifying a general locale but allowing free rein to his (and his readers') imagination when it comes down to specific details.

Naturally, for all children, ruined abbeys are bound to be the depositories of hidden treasure, and a book which starts with a bird's eye view illustration of the local landscape gives each reader the chance to follow the search for clues as the Blake children, Caroline and Andrew, attempt to trace the 'footprints' mentioned in the title. The book's illustrator is Shirley Hughes, and the landscape of the Abbey Tower, the Toll Bridge (the Blakes' new home), the Old Mill, the mushroom field, the winding course of the mysterious river and the narrow road are all laid out for our inspection.

Like so many of William Mayne's books (more often set in the Yorkshire Dales), water is at the centre of the story and the mystery. Other more conventional plot devices emerge. There is the runaway schoolboy who is living rough; there is the malevolent villain whose basic prickly character and rooted dislike of children mask the deeper greed that motivates his actions. There is even the local policeman whose activities are more likely to hinder the children in their quest than frustrate the real criminals. Thrown in amongst this is the sheer quirkiness of the writer's invention. So we have, for example, the runaway boy, Stephen Feast, adopting the alias of Wenceslas because of the carol about the feast of Stephen. Character is also carefully delineated in dialogue that brings people vividly to life. The children's father seems to live his life uttering wry observations about people and places. Another striking success is the villain, Squenn, whose every word seems to consist of a warning, a reproach or a threat. There is also the anxious uncle of the missing boy, who feels he needs to practise his ability to talk to children because it just won't come naturally.

This is not a straightforward treasure-finding adventure, though any reader would be satisfied with the ways the strands of the plot have been drawn together. It is an attempt to enter into the complex, worrying, yet sometimes magic world of younger children. It is the first of many by this author who eventually gained the Carnegie Medal for his unusual representations of childhood in *A Grass Rope*.

A Modern Comedy
A contrast to the otherworldliness of Mayne's book is **The Exiles (13)** by Hilary McKay, first published in 1993. In this first book of a modern trilogy, the four girls of the Conroy family, who are aged from six to thirteen, do not want to go to Cumbria. Cumbria is where Big Grandma lives and Big Grandma doesn't like them. Clues to the exact location of her house are left unclear, but we know that it is near the Irish Sea coast, in sight of a railway station and has a two-thousand-foot-high hill almost in the back garden. For Phoebe, Rachel, Naomi and Ruth it is in the middle of nowhere, and, worst of all, there are no books in the house for them to read. The summer holidays stretch out implacably before them, and Big Grandma closes in relentlessly on what she considers to be the world's most spoiled children. And on the second day it starts to rain. Trapped in the house, constantly at odds with each other and starved of books, they are forced to find new resources to amuse themselves.

It would be unfair to reveal too much more of the story of a book which is readily available from booksellers or from libraries. This is an exquisite comedy, with the four distinct personalities of the Conroys engaged in a continual clash with the woman who temporarily rules their lives.

In the Lower Hills
Quite a few of Showell Styles' books for children are to do with mountaineering, and one can read with some enjoyment the way in which his knowledge of the physical details of climbing and his understanding of the psychology of climbers are cleverly integrated into the plausible plots which he creates. The Lake District is not one of his

usual venues, and *The Camp in the Hills* **(14)**, published in 1964 in the Benn Bandit series of books, is for younger children, where he cannot display the full range of his capabilities.

Having mentioned these reservations, it is fair to say that the book probably meets its audience's requirements because of some of Mr Styles' other skills. The location is fictional, but the terrain described to the reader is made real both by the uncluttered and easy-to-read sketch map and by the pellucid clarity of the descriptions. The villains are villains, and it doesn't give away too much of the plot if I reveal that a kidnap is involved.

The Camp in the Hills would certainly prove a very satisfactory stepping

The four campers discuss the mystery
(illustration by Graham Coton).

stone for younger children on their way into the great world of mystery and adventure that can open before them as they grow older. The historical novels of Julian Atterton provide a good example of this development.

The Elusive Quests of Simon de Falaise

The plot of *Knights of the Lost Domain* **(15)** by Julian Atterton, published in 1991, takes the newly-knighted Simon all over the lawless Cumbria of the reign of King Stephen on a mission for Thurstan, Archbishop of York. Simon is charged with accompanying a noble lady, Maud de Romilly, to her home in the frequently ravaged land of the west coast in the aftermath of the war between the Scots and the English. It is not a journey he relishes.

It was a passage lined with bones. On every side were scorch-marks that had once been villages.

From a small fortress in the south Cumberland town of Millom (see map, page xvi), they move past Ravenglass to the blackened remains of Calder Abbey. Everywhere are the signs of the Scots, and the reader feels the almost palpable threat of the villain Fitzduncan.

Egremont Castle, whose ruins can easily be seen today, is on the brink of surrender.

> At the heart of the desolation stood the castle, its tall Norman keep-tower looking out over a land stripped bare. Here even the trees had been cut down. It was as if a dragon had come and blasted the land with fire, and the castle alone had endured.

Even a glimpse of nearby Wast Water only deepens the feeling of horror.

> We turned inland—into a dale that must have been carved at the dawn of time by the slash of a giant's axe, within the hollow of its trough a long and narrow lake as blue as sapphire and as deep as sorrow.

Yet Atterton's story also manages to suggest its awesome beauty:

> On the far side of Wast Water there was not even a track; the lake lapped like a moat against sheer screes that fanned down from crags as tall as cathedrals.

The doomed Egremont Castle

For a while, however, the next stage of this gripping narrative must be postponed. You can find the next episode of Simon's quest on page 117 in Chapter VII, as it moves to a climax near to Derwentwater.

The Tales of Ravenglass

It is fair to say that chronologically, the children's story history of the region begins with the Romans. It also begins with one of the best writers and one of the most exciting plots. *Word to Caesar* (16) by Geoffrey Trease, published in 1955, has its origin in the deepest Lake District. It is set high up on the fells just by Hardknott Fort at the head of the Hardknott Pass. It begins with the most normal of human activities—a fifteen-year-old boy paying his attentions to a pretty young girl. However, it also begins with a betrayal that is to place young Paul in immediate danger and then to change his whole way of life. The Roman emperor of the time is Trajan, who is depicted as a harsh man who intends to hold on to every scrap of land that has been conquered by the armies. Even the high peaks of the Lake District in the remote province of Britain must be held against all possible enemies. However, discipline at Hardknott has been allowed to go slack, and Paul's father, recently transferred to the remote outpost just before his release from the army as a time-served soldier, knows that things are not as they ought to be.

It is a lonely time for Paul as he waits for the days to pass until his father gets his discharge. Slipping out of the fort to meet the girl he calls Barbara proves to have many attractions. She listens to all he has to say, hanging on his every word as he describes the position of the soldiers inside the fort and the easy and unseen ways in and out. Flattered by her attentions, he says far more than is prudent. Little does he realise that the northern tribes have planned a rising in force and that he is helping to provide a key to the Romans' defeat.

Geoffrey Trease conveys brilliantly the harsh and lonely beauty of the hills, but does not dwell for long on the details before he plunges the reader into following Paul on a headlong flight for his life as the tribesmen break in, slaughter the guards and set the place on fire. Paul is saved because he is in the bath-house at the time. However, his respite is only temporary and his escape is only ensured by the sacrifice of his father's orderly, Gito, as he attempts to cross a fast-rushing stream. Then all that is left to Paul is the road to Ravenglass and an attempt to save the next Roman settlement from similar destruction. His father is dead and he is unsure of the extent of the responsibility he must bear for the fate of Hardknott.

 Hardknott Fort can still be visited by the determined walker or by the driver who feels like tackling the challenging Hardknott Pass. Beware of underestimating how arduous this journey can be, for there are one-in-three gradients and many hairpin bends. In most places there is only room for one car to get past at a time.

Once you have arrived, however, you can immediately see why a

Roman soldier would regard Mediobogdum (its Roman name) as one of the bleakest postings in the whole of the Empire. Walk five minutes over some boggy ground from the road and you can enter the remains of the fort. Look out of the north gate and, on a clear day, Scafell looms to threaten you. The eerie ruins of gateways, corner towers, interval towers and store-houses are all around you. The baths, with a clear layout of three rooms, can be seen outside the main walls. It is even possible to detect an area of flattened ground that is believed to be where the conscripts did their parade practice. High on its rocky spur, the fort offers a spectacular set of views and conjures up a vivid picture of that secure bastion that Paul believed he had betrayed to the deceitful Barbara.

Look down the road to the west. It is hard to imagine anyone running non-stop nearly ten miles to Ravenglass. Take care if you decide to drive further in the opposite direction, for you will soon realise that the Wrynose Pass, which eventually leads to the road to Ambleside, is full of its own perils for the unwary motorist.

Ravenglass also brings us to the work of Rosemary Sutcliff, whose two tales of the Lake District mark her out as the most compelling of historical novelists. *The Shield Ring* (107) (page 145) takes us to the secret heart of Lakeland and must come later. *Sword Song* (17), published in 1997, belongs very much to this coast and, at first at least, to Ravenglass.

It is in the days of the Scandinavian immigrants that *Sword Song* begins, in Ravenglass. In fact it begins in the hall of the man who gave his name to the place, Rafn the Chief. In front of Rafn Cedricson is a sixteen-year-old youth, Bjarni, who is awaiting the judgement of the man who will decide his destiny. The charge against him is that he has killed a man, in fact an itinerant priest of the White Christ, in a petty quarrel about a dog. In Rafn's land-take such a thing is prohibited, for Rafn's foster brother has become a Christian, and, out of love for him, Rafn has sworn an oath that priests of that religion should be safe. As he hears the old story, Bjarni realises that it is no longer a question of judgement but of sentence. For the reader, banishment for such an awful crime might seem unusually light, but for Bjarni it is the end of the world he knows. Bravely, he tells his elder brother Gram not to accompany him as he goes into his five-year exile. On his way to the ship that will take him and his sword out into the world to earn his living, Bjarni stops in a little valley that no one has yet claimed and buries his most precious possession, a blue glass dolphin, in the earth.

The bulk of this story tells of Bjarni's journeys around the Irish Sea and the different sets of allegiances and friendships that he develops. It is also, of course, about his growth to maturity. When he returns, five years later, he has understood the appeal of Christianity and has discovered love in the form of a Welsh girl whom he has rescued from accusations of witchcraft. He has a message of forgiveness and peace for Rafn, and a keen desire to settle on his own homestead in the little valley that leads to the hills. The clashing appeals of adventure and settlement, and thus of war and peace, have all been skilfully presented in way that explains the seeming contradiction of the Northmen's virtues and vices.

The real Ravenglass of today contains the traces of some of the features that made it a vital fortified headquarters in Roman times. It clearly was an ideal naval base, for the three rivers, the Esk, the Mite and the Irt, all converge to create great curving estuaries with excellent protection from onshore winds. The Romans called their fort here by the name of Glannaventa, and it is possible to take a short, well-signposted walk to the remains of the bath-house with its twelve-foot-high walls, still sheltering on the edge of a belt of trees. Once a market town with its own charter granted in 1208, Ravenglass used to be a thriving settlement where local farmers sold their produce. Today it has an old-fashioned atmosphere and a peculiar faded charm. The celebrated train 'La'al Ratty', at the Ravenglass and Eskdale Railway, is a vigorous survivor from the age of steam, and, after many years of carrying minerals from the mountains, is now a fascinating tourist railway attraction that can take you part of the way up the valley of the Esk.

'La'al Ratty'—the Ravenglass and Eskdale Railway heads up the Esk Valley near Eskdale Green Station (photographer: Ken Cservenka).

It is time to give a brief mention to Julian Atterton's other Lakeland book, ***Knights of the Sacred Blade*** **(18)**, published in 1989. This first story of Simon's adventures in the north of England is primarily set in Northumbria, but also has its minor western Lakeland scenes, including a journey to Carlisle and a period of imprisonment in its grim castle. However, the evocation of the Cumbrian people and places is at its most intense elsewhere, as we shall see in the Ullswater section of Chapter VIII on page 136.

Brazil in the North—a Girls' School Adventure

It is a tremendous jump in both time and mood to approach the work of the famous girls' school story writer Angela Brazil, and her book ***Three Terms at Uplands*** **(19)**, published in 1945. However, the change illustrates very clearly the qualities of an author like Julian Atterton who brings the landscape alive by the sheer meticulousness of his detail and his imaginative reconstruction of the past, as compared to the appeal of a writer like Brazil who 'borrows' the Cumbrian landscape in general for certain key episodes in the lives of her young schoolgirls.

The heroine of *Three Terms at Uplands* is called Claire Johnston, and she was born in Keswick in the Lake District. This fact about her birth is one of the cornerstones of the plot, for it proves to be the route to her school at Uplands and thus eventually to her chance for happiness. It all starts when a senior prefect at her state high school in Monkaster shows Claire an advertisement worded as follows:

> The Johnston Scholarship at Uplands School for Girls near Braith-on-Sea, Westmorland, will be vacant in September. Candidates must bear the name of Johnston, must have been born in Westmorland, and have attained the age of thirteen years in July. Full particulars from the Headmistress.

Claire qualifies in all respects. This opportunity means a lot to her, for, as an orphan girl with very little money in the family, she has almost no chance of a superior education.

Uplands is meant to be on the western edge of the Lake District. When eventually Claire sets off in October, the author gives us very few hints as to the actual locality. The journey northwards is taken by rail.

> After passing through some uninteresting country they at last reached a prospect of distant hills on the one side and glimpses of the sea on the other, and finally arrived at the little town of Braith, where a taxi had been ordered and was waiting to take them to Uplands, some miles away.

Thus the story is clearly set on the west coast of Cumbria, and the railway journey is on the line that leads eventually to Carlisle. I must sound a word of caution, however. The ancient county of Westmorland was entirely landlocked—the name of Braith-on-Sea is thus rendered impossible from the start.

Claire comes to the school late, as so many other heroines have had to do. Moreover, the author introduces a new complication to the old standard awkwardness of trying to fit in after everyone else has started. This is in the character of Ethel Johnson (note the different spelling of the surname). Ethel used to attend Claire's old school in Monkaster and was always a bit of a troublemaker. When she learned of Claire's idea of getting the scholarship and going to Uplands, she became intrigued by the idea herself. And so when Claire arrives she learns that Ethel has been at Uplands since September and established herself as one of the 'Johnnies' because of the coincidence of her name, although she is, in fact, a fee-paying pupil. Claire, to her well-concealed horror and disappointment, is branded as Ethel's friend and is allocated a bed in the same room as the girl she hoped to escape. Pretty soon, Ethel's attempts at having a little fun rebound not on that young maiden but on poor Claire, who finds herself the object of the senior girls' distrust and dislike. She is very far from their idea of what the 'Johnston Scholarship' girl ought to be.

Ironically, Claire, though not tremendously bright in the academic field, is truly appreciative of the education she is receiving and is sensitive to the tragic circumstances that have led to her getting a chance at the school. The scholarship had been set up by a grieving father in memory of his daughter who had drowned in the sea. The dangers of being cut off by the tide on this coast are well illustrated by the previous chapter in this book. With details reminiscent of the Morecambe Bay coast—'The rising tide flowed in at a most amazing pace, covering the sands in an incredibly short time, and in the course of a few minutes filling the little bays'—Angela Brazil inevitably constructs a brief episode in which Claire's quick thinking averts a second tragic death.

The book ends with an almost-impossible-to-contemplate coincidence which has been well telegraphed from Chapter 1 and which concerns a mine in Mexico. However, the charm of the story comes almost entirely from the episodes in which Claire copes with Ethel and makes friends with most of her classmates.

The St Vivians Quartet

Another elusive girls' school appears in the series of four stories by Patricia Caldwell, which began in 1956. This establishment is called St Vivians, and it lies a twenty-minute walk from the village of 'Garth', about two miles from the Cumberland coast. The small town of 'Rosley', which boasts its own theatre, is a mere seven miles further away. Alas, once again all these names are fictitious and thus any investigation of the setting leads to no firm conclusion.

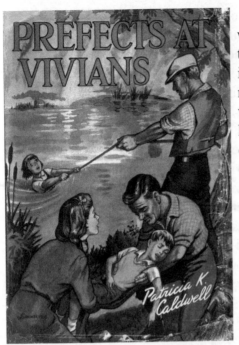

However, to dwell any further on the point would be to exaggerate the importance of the landscape in books which are so clearly inward looking. What happens in school is what matters, and each book is a subtle study of the workings of the prefects, the head girl and the headmistress, all operating in a closed, almost claustrophobic, atmosphere. *Prefects at Vivians* **(20)** is concerned with Lesley Trevor, the newly appointed prefect who must overcome her reluctance to assume a leading role in the management of the other girls. Chris Rivers, the head girl, together with her best friend Pat Meredith, make up, with Lesley, a trio of intelligent, good-hearted and hard-working young women, whose struggles with troublemakers are complicated by misunderstandings and by their own erratic progress towards knowing themselves. In *Head Girl at Vivians* **(21)** Pat and Chris have departed to higher education and Lesley must continue her endeavours alone, the situation now being complicated by an unsympathetic temporary headmistress and by an outbreak of selfish and unreasonable behaviour amongst a set of girls in a lower form. The situation ends with expulsions and a dramatic swimming competition.

Certainly the most outward-looking book in the series is *Strangers at Vivians* **(22)**, where there seems to be an almost painful awakening to the problems of the real world. The narrative focus is shifted from the doings of the prefects to the behaviour and feelings of girls on every level in the school. The influx of twenty-seven new pupils of all ages from a recently defunct school in Morecambe causes a series of events which leads to a feud breaking out between the old Vivians characters and the perceived interlopers. Most interesting of all is the arrival of Eva Mihaly, a Hungarian refugee, who, after the death of her family in the uprising against the Russians, climbed over the mountains to escape to Austria. From there, she was sent to Lancashire where there was a need for workers in the cotton mills. Through the influence of Hugh Trevor, the brother of Lesley from the first two Vivians stories, Eva is sponsored by her firm to spend two years at the boarding school. Whilst the feud begins to gather pace in the school, Eva begins to adjust to her new life. Another interesting narrative thread is followed as the author relates the experiences of Nanette Cardew, who is trying very hard to live down the reputation her family acquired when her sister was expelled the previous year. Some of the new girls with lingering fond memories of their old school are allowed a sentimental journey back to the empty premises, which convinces them that it is time to move on with their lives. The change in Eva is more dramatic and, at last, involves the landscape.

'It's strange that Vivians never spent time in the Lakes, living so close,' mused Geraldine.

With this sentiment I would agree. Towards the end of the book, the scholars at the school are finally released into the countryside that has been in their backyard since the beginning of the saga. And it is now to real places that the expeditions are sent. There is a hike across the fells from Eskdale to Wast Water. Another group are going on Coniston and, anticipating the author of this book, Linnie comments: 'I'm going to try to work out the places described in Swallows and Amazons.'

The First Formers are set to walk round Rydal Water and Grasmere and the most experienced Sixth Formers to walk up Harter Fell and to descend to the Roman Fort on Hardknott Pass. It is this final expedition that brings back Eva's nightmares of the climb out of Hungary. Eva's determination to continue to the top in spite of her memories and her fears is a reflection of her attitude to her whole life.

It only takes the fourth volume to complete the standard set of situations which encapsulate nearly all the main themes in girls' school stories. In *Left until Called for at Vivians* (23), published in 2003, Alison Cameron is an orphan new girl thrust into an alien environment by uncaring and distant relations. The mystery about her past and the fragility of the friendships she forms are gradually explored throughout the book. A perverse fate seems to mar her happiness, and the author explores new ways of creating the tensions that will engage the sympathy of the reader. Among the excursions taken by the girls during February is one by train to Grange-Over-Sands. There is a reference to the dangers of the quicksand and the Guide's house at Kent's Bank. There is then the 'easy walk up the steep streets and over Hampsfell to the village of Cartmel'. One day Alison makes a further journey northwards to Annan on the Scottish side of the Solway Firth. Here she discovers some elements of her past and gets on the trail of an older girl who had been so kind to her when she was living in the children's home there. That this older girl should prove to be one of the central characters of the first Vivians books, who is now about to be married in the local church, demonstrates the craftsmanship the author shows in bringing to a successful end not just this book but the whole quartet of gentle and rewarding narratives.

They Came from the North—the Solway Coast
Now it is time to turn to two stories where the arrival on the scene of characters from the north—some friendly and some not so—illuminates several of the features of the Solway Coast.

The first half of *The Droving Lad* (24) by Kathleen Fidler, published in 1955, is spent in Scotland, where we follow the adventures of young Colin Cameron as he and his elder brother guide their prize bull and the herd of 'stirks' to the Falkirk Tryst in order to sell them. The year is 1813 and their journey takes them through many lonely places, such as Rannoch Moor, before they arrive at their destination. It isn't just the remoteness of the terrain that causes dangers to cross their path, for the beasts that they have accepted as a solemn trust from their injured father are prizes that many robbers would be delighted to steal. Both unexpected enemies and even more surprising allies cause their journey to be considerably livelier than even the imaginative Colin had anticipated.

Mr Barlow, the farmer from near Penrith who buys their cattle, is a man who thoroughly deserves his reputation for honesty and fair dealing. The bargain that is struck between Colin and Barlow reflects credit on both parties and demonstrates that not all encounters between the English and Scots are characterised by mistrust and deception.

Having sold the herd, Colin and his brother Angus then undertake to deliver them safely to Barlow's farm. They must carry the money from the sale with them, and this means the journey south continues to be perilous. In order to avoid the tolls on two bridges after Gretna, they decide to cross the Solway between Dornock and Bowness on the Cumberland shore. The author ensures that the ordinary complications of crossing the Dornock Wath are intensified by the sudden descent of an all-enveloping mist. Her description of the perils that nearly overwhelm the two brothers and their helpers is matched by the vividness of Geoffrey Whittam's illustration as the cattle mill around in the water in a frenzy of confusion.

Further adventures await them on the Solway shore. To Colin, the city of Carlisle is

the biggest town he has ever seen in his life, and his breath is taken away by the Cathedral and the shops. Unfortunately, as well as holding many attractions, it is also the place where the robbers who dogged their trail finally catch up with them again. After a lucky escape both Simon and Colin return to the herd, and the journey onwards to Catterlen, near Penrith, is undertaken by the most remote routes that their old herdsman, Donald, can devise.

A warning from the gypsy girl whom Colin had rescued back on Rannock Moor sends them on their way for the final part of the adventure. This includes their encounter with a travelling group of players, and performances in Penrith, Keswick, Cockermouth, and then, most significantly from the point of view of this section of our travels, at Maryport.

The herd crosses the Bowness Channel as the Solway Bore rushes in (illustration by Geoffrey Whittam).

'Maryport proved a little town of mean houses where black-faced miners dwelt.' It is also the place where all the key ingredients of the plot come together to create the climax, which involves a panic-stricken flight, a crucial error of judgement on the sea front and the vital loss of all the money from the sale at Falkirk. Everything that Colin and Angus have striven for would seem to be wasted—they must return to their father in shame and humiliation. However, the good faith of one young girl brings about the surprising happy ending. The cunning way in which the story has been told, as reminiscence, produces yet another.

***Master Deor's Apprentice* (25)** by M A Wood, published in 1977, takes us back to a much earlier period.

When Kenny leaves his home in the borderlands of England and Scotland, he is driven on by the thought that he is not destined to spend all of his days as a field worker, carrying manure for another man's crops. Something in the magic beauty of a Celtic cross, as it reflects the rays of the setting sun, has inspired him to make what is, for him, an epic journey. Kenny is determined to seek out the famous stonemason, Master Deor, who lives near the site of the modern town of Maryport, and become his apprentice. The story is partly about his pilgrimage to find the man, and his struggles to be accepted amongst the small community of boys who are learning their craft, near to the perilous waters of the Solway Firth almost a thousand years ago.

In a way, this book also represents one of the earliest settings for a school story, for the second half of the book is about the way the young boy learns to adapt himself to the workshop amongst his fellow apprentices who contain the usual selection of bullies, weaklings and decent young men. His talent and determination will ensure his ultimate success, but not before great excitement and some danger have entered his life.

In Maryport today it is easy to imagine how the redeveloped quay area, now an attractive place to visit, was once the grim and grimy home to the many boats and ships transporting coal from the mines in the surrounding area. Kathleen Fidler's droving lad's desperate pier-head leap as his pursuers closed in on him that moonlit night could be from any of the wharves you can see around you.

It is possible to trace this industrial aspect of the town's history in a specialised steamship museum and a more generalised maritime museum. However, a trip into the more distant past, close to the world of Kenny the apprentice, can be taken by climbing up to the cliff above the promenade. Next to Hadrian's Cycleway, you will find the remains of the Roman fort of Alauna.

Kenny's destination, Master Deor's workshop, is depicted as being some two to three miles inland from Maryport at the village of Dearham. The modern village (the author makes her hero the inspiration for its name) still contains relics of a pre-Norman cross standing at the west end of the church. The Dearham Nordic cross tells in miniature the story of this period of pagan overlap which is the background to the story of Kenny and his desire to become a mason. Odin and his messenger ravens are sculpted at the foot of the shaft, while the words 'Ash Yggdrasil' (the World Tree spanning heaven and hell) rise from the base to weave their way up to the Christian Celtic wheel cross at the top.

The young boy's longing to become a mason first began at the Bewcastle Cross, which is to be found much further north in Cumbria. Visiting this location involves a long but interesting expedition from the A69 Carlisle to Newcastle road, through Brampton, across Hadrian's Wall, past Lanercost Priory and up a sharp hill to Bewcastle Church and the extraordinary cross. On this journey to the outer limits of Cumbria and England, you too will pass some key elements of the surroundings that so impressed the young boy in search of a vocation: the formidable traces of the Roman occupation, the haunting symbols of worship of the Norse gods, and the rugged but beautiful isolated Christian churches that still seem to defy the loneliness of the hills near the Scottish border. For those fascinated by the strange blend of Nordic and Christian crosses, a journey through Carlisle and westwards into Dumfries and Galloway will take you to the other side of the Solway Firth and a chance to see perhaps the most extraordinary of all the stone crosses at Ruthwell, site of one of the oldest preaching crosses in Europe.

An Abbeytown Story

In the second book by M A Wood, *The Year the Raiders Came* (26), published in 1977, we experience a year in the life of David, an abandoned orphan in the fifteenth century who lives in the shadow of St Mary's Abbey (present-day Abbeytown) near the River Waver. The author traces his passage through the four seasons, from the 'flock-gathering' of summer, through the frightening Scottish raid during the late summer and early autumn, to his miserable existence during the cruelty of a frozen winter and the advent of a stormy and life-threatening spring. It is a year which is to change the course of young David's whole existence.

David is given by the monks of the Abbey to the local flockmaster. Here he is treated appallingly, starved of food and set to do all the dirty jobs. One evening, though not suited to the calling of herd-boy, he is a true Good Shepherd and nearly sacrifices his life to save a sheep that has got stuck in the mud of the estuary. The kind-hearted Brother John and the severe but just Brother Dominic give him a new start by passing him over to the household of the local craftsman in wood.

For the first time in his life he finds friends, in the craftsman's son Robin and another orphan, a poor girl called Margery, whose prize possession is a goose called Esmeralda. However, Garath, the flockmaster's son, is both spiteful and malicious and tries to ensure by his constant bullying that none of them have any happiness or peace. Worse than that, the little village is subjected to a surprise border raid by the Scots, who are believed to be led by a horrific disfigured man called Nebless Nick Armstrong. The fear and danger nearly overwhelm the three children, but in spite of this, young Margery insists that the Scots, though harsh and greedy in their thefts from the village, are not monsters but people just like them.

Although this is a short book written for younger children of eight to eleven years, it gives a convincing picture of what life could be like for a small boy in medieval times in a remote village on the Solway Firth.

 Always in the background of the story is the Abbey. Though dedicated to St Mary, it has been known throughout the ages as Holm Cultram Abbey.

You too can visit what has survived more than eight centuries of turbulent history. In the quiet village of Abbeytown it is easy to park quite near to the unusual church. The building that rises up before you today is the product of much restoration, but it is still possible to admire the wonderful Norman arch of the west doorway and the fine arcade of pillars in the side walls. After admiring the magnificent oak beams of the interior, retreat to the churchyard, sit on the carefully tended grass outside and try to recapture the image of a building that was once even bigger than Carlisle Cathedral and which had a community of Cistercian monks who believed that 'to work was to pray'. Before you leave, seek out the modern grave memorial which reminds you that even today this site can reach out and touch those who live in the district.

It is sad to report that since I wrote these words there has been a

Wast Water (photographer: Peter Lewis)

31

devastating fire at the abbey. All but one of the stained glass windows have been saved. The magnificent east window is largely undamaged, as is the annexe which houses most of the important grave slabs and carvings. It is still worth a visit.

***The Secret Tarn* (27)** by J L Rallings, published in 1962, is another very short book of ninety-six pages where an author tries to trace how the influence of religion can change the lives of even very young children.

It belongs in this section of the book because the tarn of the title lies not far from the Wasdale home of the young heroine's Aunt Mary. As she is driven towards the farm by her cousin Jim, Jenny gets her first impressions of Wast Water:

> The narrow road wound along the lake side, and Jenny could see the water, dark and deep below them. Great black hills rose up on the other side. She shivered suddenly.
>
> 'I told you this was the most exciting lake of all, didn't I?' said Jim. 'Those black hills are called the Screes. It is their reflection that makes the water so dark, even on a sunny day, like this. No one has ever discovered how deep it is.'

Dick rescues his chum Jimmy from a burning room (illustration by Murray Urquhart).

The early promise of this description is not fulfilled because of the vagueness of the narrative that follows. In essence *The Secret Tarn* proves to be a totally predictable Sunday school story from the religious publishers Pickering and Inglis.

***In a Hand of Steel* (28)** by Paul Creswick, published in 1907, has many of the hallmarks of one sort of story that used to appear in the popular magazine *Boy's Own Paper* during the first thirty years of its existence. Young boys on the threshold of adult life grapple with mysteries of the adult world involving exotic foreigners, strange bequests in wills and settings in wild and largely unspecific countryside both in Great Britain and abroad. The construction of such stories is largely episodic, with cliff-hangers being provided to get the readership to come back the following week or month to see how the dangerous situation is resolved. Character development is minimal and the motivation of the villains is most generally attributed to natural malevolence or to revenge for the wrongs committed by a previous generation. The British boys concerned always display the requisite amount of pluck and determination, and a tangible treasure is often the reward in the last chapter.

The boys' pursuit of the wicked Diego leads to the small, and real, village of Boot. For several chapters the author has his characters travelling to and fro on trains between Boot and Ravenglass with vital incidents taking place on different platforms at either end of the line. At one point Dick and Jimmy, the heroes, even steal a train and run it in an exhilarating fashion through the stations at Eskdale Green, Irton Road and Muncaster. Surely this must be the most dramatic story that La'al Ratty (see pages 23 and 171) has ever featured in! The totally mysterious casket is finally opened on the platform of Boot Station and the contents are revealed:

> … lying upon a padded leather cushion, strangely strapped with steel bands
> to prevent its shifting, was the presentment, in rusty iron, of a human hand
> horridly cut off at the wrist.

The twists and turns of the plot are not finished with yet, but the author returns for his final sensational climax into that other unspecific Lake District with its stock features of beetling crags, unfathomable abysses and sucking marshes that are so convenient for desperate encounters and the disposal of dead bodies. Neither the dastardly Diego nor the treacherous tutor escapes his much-deserved fate. An act of charity disposes of both the treasure and the curse; and the clenched 'hand of steel' is opened, to everyone's satisfaction. It is time for us to recover our breath and move on. This extraordinary tale of fantastic adventure and 'derring-do', like several of the other books so far, such as *The Mystery Prize*, *Knights of the Lost Domain*, *Word to Caesar* and *The Droving Lad*, has merely given us a glimpse of the heartlands to come.

The first step on our way there will be to the extraordinary place called Bannermere.

BANNERMERE AND THE TARN

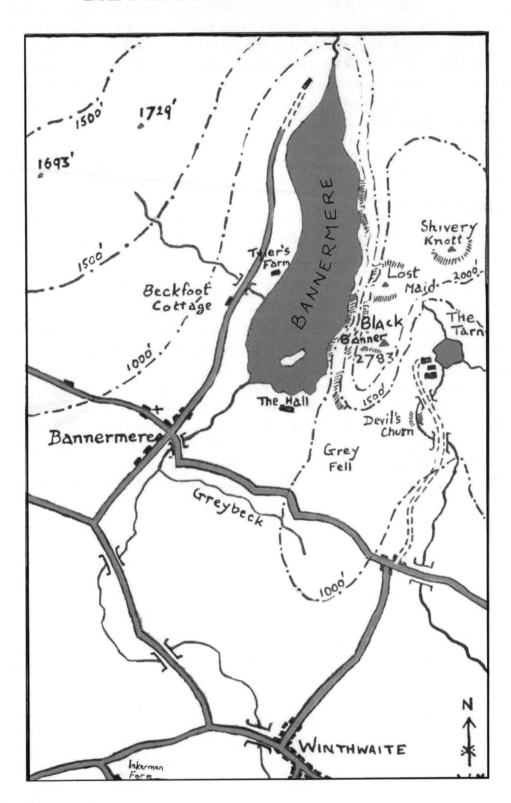

CHAPTER III

THE BANNERMERE NOVELS
Wast Water, Eskdale, the Jaws of Borrowdale, Gosforth, Cockermouth

'It isn't far as the crow flies, but the mountains get in the way, and we have
to go round them.'

THESE words from *The Secret Tarn* (see page 32) sum up the next landscape perfectly.
    The valley of Wasdale is often described as the 'hidden corner' of the Lake District.
Unless you are a determined walker or climber, the road that runs alongside the often
gloomy-looking Wast Water seems to lead nowhere. Ahead, you are confronted by
dramatic scenery with Great Gable and Scafell Pike dominating the views beyond the
head of the lake, and, looming up on your right, the extraordinary screes present at
some times an intimidating wall of shadow and menace and at others a shimmering
coloured canvas of reflected sunlight. By road from Keswick, Kendal or Windermere
the journey does indeed seem a long and roundabout one. Yet for the author at the
centre of this chapter it was always one which was well worth taking. For it was precisely
this scenery that inspired most of the settings for Bannermere.
    The five books of the Bannermere series by Geoffrey Trease, published between
1949 and 1954, produce the most complete and detailed picture of family life to be
found in children's fiction set in the Lake District. You will detect in the preceding
sentence my own admiration and liking for these particular stories by my favourite
children's author.
    As the stories have recently been republished, it would hardly be fair to reproduce
too many details of the plots in the description which follows. Frankly, in my opinion,
the books are simply too good to spoil them for any potential readers, whether they be
children or adults. Let us begin with brief outlines of some of the ingredients in the
tales and a quick view of the gallery of characters.

A Gallery of Characters
Bill tells each of the stories, but the last thing you would call him is an omniscient
narrator. Sometimes it is clear that the slowly maturing Bill has neither much of a clue
about what is going on around him, nor a full appreciation of other people's feelings.
    What strikes us most about Bill is his decency and his good humour. He loves
literature, especially plays, and comes to develop a particular affection for the
countryside around Bannermere. Some of his efforts to become a writer draw upon
Trease's own experiences of struggle and failure and the need to find an individual

artistic integrity. We share his setbacks and his triumphs, his hopes and his fears, not just in his literary endeavours but also when his deeper feelings are involved.

At one point Bill declares that his sister Susan is a much nicer person than he is. Though a year younger than her brother, Susan comes to understand much more quickly what she wants from the world and which people are going to be most important to her. The life of the countryside has an overwhelming appeal for her, and this comes out not just in her interest in farming but in her knowledge of wildlife and the local people.

The heroine of the series is undoubtedly Penelope Morchard. Penny's physical appearance is mentioned many times during the course of the novels. Three things are bound to remain in our memories—her dark hair, the smooth perfection of her skin and the look of mischief in her dark eyes. Of course, we also remember her limp, the result of a childhood accident that has apparently blighted her life. The route to maturity is hardest for Penny of all the four children whom we meet in *No Boats on Bannermere*. Her talent for acting, her natural vivacity and her passionate nature cannot always dispel the feeling of gloom that overwhelms her when she considers how she might have been a success on the stage. In some ways her access to all the books in her father's shop and the lively discussions she has with her affectionate parent have made her older than her years. In other ways she is a prey to her sudden enthusiasms, which lead her into foolishness, and this teaches her the harsh lessons of this world. Each member of the Melbury family eventually brings her something she has never had before in her life, but to tell more would spoil the story of the books.

Tim Darren's ambition to be a detective is at the core of his character. He is always sensible and patient in his approach to all the problems and mysteries that they encounter. He represents solid Cumbrian common sense—in particular we remember the advice he gives Bill and the others about safe behaviour whilst out on the fells.

Inevitably his slowness and 'plodding' occasionally lay him open to the ridicule of the others. However, he laughs at himself and confesses that the police in the district treat him warily because of previous examples of his misplaced zeal. His future is mapped out in a plausible and satisfactory manner—making another contrast with the insecurity that lies ahead for both Bill and Penny.

Bill with an open book in the foreground,
Tim with his thumb keeping his place,
Susan with a paper bag and Penny smiling
at the back
(illustration by Richard Kennedy)

Left: Winter in Winthwaite. Bill, Penny and Mr Morchard wait for the last bus to
Bannermere on Christmas Eve.
Right: Tim rescues the passengers from Miss Florey's trapped car.
(Illustrations by Richard Kennedy)

A Variety of Plots

In *No Boats on Bannermere* **(29)**, Bill and Susan find themselves in the traditional
role of the newcomer. Transplanted from the south of England to a lonely cottage in
Cumberland, they have to adapt to a new home and school, and to the new friends that
they make. When they stumble on the trail of an ancient mystery and fall foul of the
local landowner who issues the interdict 'No boats on Bannermere', the story develops
to involve Vikings, aerial photographs, a dead body and the respective (and respected)
Heads of their two schools.

Under Black Banner **(30)** takes an issue that might be considered to be frozen in
time but which, in reality, is still of high concern to many people in rural districts
today. The farm near Black Banner Tarn was requisitioned by the Government for
army training during the Second World War. Now that the hostilities have long since
passed, the land and the cottages on it languish in neglect, no longer used by the military
but unable to be reclaimed by the family.

While Bill and his friends take on the dead hand of bureaucracy, Trease also develops
the more everyday aspects of the relationships between the major characters. Bill is
forced to watch Penny get involved with a boy whom he detests, and Susan feels the
first stirring of feeling for a young man in the district.

By the time of *Black Banner Players* **(31)**, the emphasis of the series has shifted very strongly to the personal lives of Bill, Penny and Susan. Each is now old enough to look to the future, and the author carefully depicts how these teenagers in the small Lakeland community try to come to terms with both success and failure, with friendship and affection. The pictures of the Winthwaite and Bannermere surroundings in winter are particularly striking. Another mystery presents itself to be solved, and Trease conjures up some wholly convincing pictures of the remoteness of some communities and the devastating effects of the weather.

Strangely enough, **Black Banner Abroad (32)**, in spite of its story of continental travel, actually provides the reader with the most convincing and moving picture of a character from Cumberland. This is Willy the Waller, who spends his life repairing the drystone walls that divide the pastures in the high fells. His wartime experiences in occupied France have left a profound impression on this simple man, who has too much time to brood over a selfish act which he committed during a time of great panic. He turns to the children to help him out, hoping against hope that they will be able to make the reparations that will ease his conscience. Bill, Penny, Tim and Susan find themselves entrusted with a task that is almost beyond their resources, but which they set about with great determination and tact. The description of the holiday of the teenagers from remote Cumberland who take their version of Romeo and Juliet to the south of France is enhanced by further changes in the core relationships, which will fascinate those readers who have invested a good deal of emotion in the likeable Bill and the stormy but talented Penny.

The last volume, **The Gates of Bannerdale (33)**, contains the essence of its theme in its title. Everyone comes to the end of their schooldays, and unless they are destined to be farmers, the young people must move out of their remote Cumbrian environment to make the next step. The author very carefully maintains a balance between the love for the world they are leaving behind and the excitement of the new land that lies outside. A good deal of confusion in the relationship between Penny and Bill means that for a long while, though together at Oxford, they face the challenges apart. Once again, as with the first book, Trease places a tangible treasure at the heart of the plot, but this time the real discovery is to do with the many things that the young people find out about the nature of truth and the importance of the feelings that they have for each other.

At the time they were written, in the late 1940s and early 1950s, the books in the series were regarded as breaking the mould of the traditional English school story. From the talks that he gave around the country, Trease had become aware that many of the children he talked to wanted stories about real children who went to real day schools. Plots about catching spies, chasing ghosts or holding midnight feasts were no longer required. Stories which involved both boys and girls, and which examined their relationships with each other as they grew up, could, he believed, prove to have a tremendous appeal. Life at day school is at the centre of all of these stories, and even the last, *The Gates of Bannerdale*, is as much about leaving home and school as it is about life at Oxford.

The Bannermere stories were once about contemporary life; now, more than fifty years later, they give an intriguing picture of the world of post-war Britain with its housing shortages, its focus on the Officer Training Corps and National Service, the lingering effect of the Second World War, and a distinct separation of behaviour and thinking between those who lived in the country and those who were town or city dwellers. There are even some brief indications of the increased breakdown of the traditional bedrock of married life. Bill and Susan Melbury live alone with their mother not because of the traditional reasons for an absent father—death in action or long service abroad in the colonies—but because the Melburys have divorced. This is conveyed to the reader in a typically understated way by Bill's first-person narrative:

> As a matter of fact, our father isn't dead. He's in Canada. Mum divorced him when we were both quite small, and, although he's supposed to send money through the lawyers, he hasn't sent any for ages, so things have been pretty difficult ever since we can remember. Still, we always get along somehow, and I believe there are thousands of families with the same kind of problem.

Such family disruption is so commonplace in children's literature today that it is difficult to realise the degree to which Trease was taking a small but important stride towards realism. Yet it would create a false picture if this account suggested that Trease abandoned many of the traditional devices and stratagems to get his readers hooked on the plots of his books. After all, *No Boats on Bannermere* is about the search for a treasure on an island in the middle of a lake. And Winthwaite Grammar School, with Mr Kingsford as its tartar of a headmaster and with its tradition for high academic standards, is, at first sight, not so far away in its ethos from the public schools that had been the backbone of stories from Talbot Baines Reed onwards. Trease's triumph is that the children in his stories carry out their investigations, and both endure and enjoy their schooldays, in worlds which feel palpably real. In fact the old truisms of plot and situation are undermined whilst still being used. Mr Kingsford, with his antiquated attitude towards his 'boys' and their interest in the opposite sex, is gradually converted to a more realistic appraisal of the way in which things will happen, whatever schoolteachers may do to

Bill and Susan take their first voyage in the *Argo* (illustration by Richard Kennedy).

exercise their control. Trease even manages both to celebrate and mock the sporting traditions of the school story by a series of set pieces that are equally enthralling and amusing: the cricket matches which resemble the chaos on the fields of Waterloo, the athletics meet where the honest Bill is outperformed by the boy who becomes his deadly rival for the affections of Penny, the final rugby match where Bill realises that the next time he has the honour of being stomped on in the mud, he will be one of the 'Old Boys'.

The nauseating Seymour runs away with the race (illustration by Richard Kennedy).

The Locations

At the heart of the books there is the landscape. Let us remember once more the broad outlines of the world that Trease describes: in remote West Cumberland the Melburys live in a small cottage called Beckfoot in the narrow valley of Bannerdale on the edge of Lake Bannermere. Across the lake, the scree-covered mountain of Black Banner rises dramatically to the sky. At the foot of the valley, beyond the little village also called Bannermere, the mountain fells, called at this point the Gates of Bannerdale, close in so that the road to the outside world seems almost cut off by a barrier. Just outside the valley is the small town of Winthwaite where both children go to school.

Can the reader really go there and see the places? In the second volume of his autobiography, *Laughter at the Door*, Geoffrey Trease reveals that:

> Bannerdale, with its lake and forbidden islet and its sombre mountain, Black Banner, lowering over it, is one of those private fantasy regions that authors, and especially children's authors, love to create.

This seems quite disappointing, but later he admits that Bannerdale is a combination of Wasdale and Eskdale, with other features 'drafted in from elsewhere'. The Jaws of Borrowdale, for example, are the inspiration for the Gates of Bannerdale. He declares that Black Banner was suggested by the slopes of Black Sail. Perhaps most importantly, the town of Winthwaite was based on Cockermouth 'shifted southwards for literary convenience'.

So how much is imagination and how much is fact? The maps provide our first clue. It is fairly straightforward to come to the conclusion that Bannermere is based upon Wast Water. However, it is a Wast Water that has been adjusted for his purposes. Use my little sketch map to compare with Trease's own map from *Under Black Banner*,

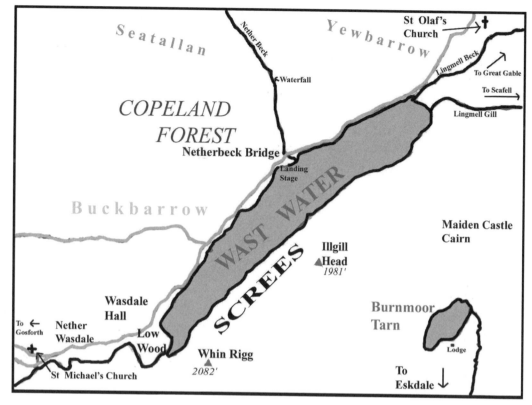

Wast Water and Burnmoor Tarn

shown at the beginning of the chapter. There you will note a long narrow lake with a tremendous set of screes down the right hand side.

Wast Water *is* a long narrow lake, known to be the deepest in England, and it has mountains running steeply down to the shore on the opposite side of the lake to where the road runs. The range of hills is backed by an area of upland in which lies Burnmoor Tarn, roughly corresponding to the position of 'The Tarn' as marked on Trease's map. A beck or stream flows into the head of Wast Water and another leaves at the bottom. Other becks flow in from the road side of the lake, and the one that emerges at Netherbeck Bridge even has waterfalls marked slightly upstream. Could this be the inspiration for Beckfoot and the cottage where Bill was woken on the first morning by the sound of falling water? There is a landing stage on the lake nearby. Is this the starting point for the voyage of their boat, the *Argo*, in *No Boats on Bannermere*?

At the foot of the lake is an area of land marked as Low Wood, and around the corner of the lake to its left is Wasdale Hall (now used as a Youth Hostel), with a thinly marked road leading to it. If these two locations were blended, we could arrive at the address of Sir Alfred Askew.

Building on this success, I might add that the location of Nether Wasdale near Wast Water corresponds to the position of Bannermere village near Bannermere Lake. Even the layout of the roads on Trease's map is not dissimilar to the position of the yellow road lines on the Ordnance Survey map.

However, you will soon notice that the real lake is not quite the right shape, nor on the correct north-south alignment, that there is no island and that the mountains are all in the wrong places.

Yet a visit to Gosforth, to Nether Wasdale, and to the banks of Wast Water is still fully justified. Turn off the A595 and pass through the small town of Gosforth. Drive on slowly to Nether Wasdale and soon you will be able to see the extraordinary wall of the screes with their perpendicular crags towering above them. On that first April morning Bill describes them as 'a great stark mountain rising almost sheer from the opposite shore, grey and mauve with a fleck of green here and there, all so bright and rain-washed that it looked like metal—or like that sheen on a pigeon's feathers'.

The colours of the screes are reputedly at their best in the winter when the russet-brown tint of the dead bracken contrasts with the red streaks of iron ore, the dark grey-brown of the crags and the green of the remaining grass. As you progress alongside the long finger of the lake, you should be able to stop at one of the small parking places and visit the possible location of Trease's Beckfoot. At the head of the lake, you enter Upper Wasdale, which is a narrow area of green fields and stone walls surrounded by a huge amphitheatre of impressive fells. Scafell Pike and its northern spur, Lingmell, are on the right; Great Gable is in front of you, and Kirkfell and Yewbarrow on your left. They may be in the wrong places for the hills surrounding Bannerdale but they are surely the right mountains.

The local Cumbrians claim that they have the deepest lake and the smallest church in England as well as the best pub and the biggest liars. You may remember that Bill confirms the depth of the lake and comments about the church: 'Bannermere people say it's the smallest in England.'

The road you follow by the side of Wast Water terminates at Wasdale Head. This is the opportunity to examine the curiously atmospheric St Olaf's, the reputed smallest church in England, which is both isolated and yet surrounded by its impressive guard of yew trees. The graveyard has the graves of climbers killed in accidents on the surrounding fells, and inside the building there is a stained glass window with a moving memorial to those members of the climbing club who died in the First World War. The church is of uncertain age but local people claim that the roof trusses were inspired by the construction of Viking longboats.

Whilst on your way out of the valley again, it is worth considering the other churches to be found nearby, which may have helped in the creation of the fictional one that plays a small part at the beginning of *No Boats on*

Bannermere and a more significant one at the end of *The Gates of Bannerdale*. There is St Michael's in Nether Wasdale, which is the right distance from the lake and is actually in the appropriately positioned hamlet which may represent Bannermere village. Don't forget St Mary's in Gosforth, whose churchyard holds the famous Viking cross mentioned in at least two of the books. Finally, after turning south on to the A595 again, consider the following description from the Eskdale web-guide of St John's Church at Waberthwaite: 'It is a simple barn-shaped building with box pews and a graveyard that in Spring defies description—a veritable carpet of colour'—which may remind you irresistibly of Bill's attempt at description of the Sunday morning at Bannermere Church. 'It's like a white-washed barn inside, but it looked beautiful that first morning, all golden with daffodils and sunshine coming in through unstained windows.'

Not one of the maps can resolve for certain just which mountain is meant to be Black Banner. The Black Sail referred to by Trease in his autobiography is a pass rather than a peak. There is little doubt, however, that the one mountain visible from Black Sail Pass which could be said to tower over Wasdale is Great Gable, and this symbol of the Lake District National Park, I suggest, is the most likely model for his fictional mountain. If you look at the background of the station scene on the cover of *The Gates of Bannerdale* and compare it with an aerial photograph of Wast Water, you will find that the shape of the distant hills in both pictures comes very close to a perfect match.

From the countryside let us now pass to the town and consider Cockermouth, which Trease identified as the model for Winthwaite.

Winthwaite—the very name suggests the ruggedness of the north, and especially the Lake District. 'Thwaite' means a piece of land cleared of trees and made into a village. 'Win' may be referring to the tenacious gorse or furze plant, or even to the activity of having to fight hard to gain the victory over the environment. Either way, it's just the right name for the small market town which greets the Melbury family as they emerge from the station. Later we learn that the town has an ancient market place, some sheep-pens, the remains of a castle, a parish church, a salmon weir and some interesting shops. On a rainy day in April, the Melbury family's preliminary impressions are almost overwhelmingly disheartening. Bill's comment seems an understatement of their feelings:

> The town centre was a long way off, we could see nothing but grey roofs and swirling gutters, and anyhow it was early-closing day.
> … We were all a bit depressed by our first glimpse of the town which was to complete our education, serve as our shopping-centre, and generally represent Civilisation for the next few years of our lives.

So far, I have suggested various explorations of the landscape, trips on foot or by car that I hope could put you in touch with the settings. It's now time to tell of one of my own attempts to walk around a location and link the fact to the fiction.

It poured with rain! I never did examine the Market Place, nor find the public library, which might have been still full of old fossils who would leap out of the shadows to screech 'Silence'. I couldn't trace Botley's where Bill enjoys the ice creams with Penny and Sue, nor track his journey back to school and the unnerving interview with Mr Kingsford about 'paying his attentions' to girls. There was indeed a Grammar School on Lorton Road near the market place in Cockermouth during Trease's time in Cumberland, but it has long since disappeared, though the public school at which the author himself taught, and from which he may also have drawn inspiration, still flourishes—but that is near Gosforth and thus in the Wasdale part of his imagined landscape. 'Typical,' I thought, 'the one day I choose to go to the place, most of my plans are frustrated by the weather.' On top of that some of the interesting shops were closed. And then it struck me—the 'grey roofs', 'swirling gutters' and the 'early-closing day'—perhaps I had been captured by the spirit of the book and had been lucky enough to visit Winthwaite after all!

 To make a definite connection with the landscape of the Bannermere novels, I suggest that the following drive would be a rewarding experience, once you have completed the exploration of the possible Wasdale, Eskdale and Cockermouth locations.

Take the B5289 out of Cockermouth and set off for Crummock Water. After the rather tame lowlands of Lorton Vale you will find the lake on your right, backed by the steeply rising Mellbreak behind. There are islands on this lake. Don't get excited—they are usually too small to be noticed unless you make a special effort to stop and look. It is better to accept that the much larger Brant Holme on Bannermere really is one of those inventions well summed up by the literary definition of the word island: 'a piece of land entirely surrounded by mystery and romance'.

The road goes on to skirt the edge of Buttermere and to tackle the Honister Pass. Then it begins the long descent into Keswick, and offers you the chance to experience the Jaws of Borrowdale which Trease used for the central symbol of *The Gates of Bannerdale*. Between the villages of Rosthwaite and Grange, the road twists and turns as the valley squeezes itself between the two molars of the jaws in the shape of Castle Crag and Grange Fell. A whole new world does open up in front of you as you catch your first sight of Derwentwater.

Bill describes the fictional Gates of Bannerdale thus:

There's a place, just beyond the village, where the dale suddenly narrows. The road runs between two crags covered with bracken and dotted with rowan trees. Those crags are called the Gates of Bannerdale, and there's an old saying: a man may go out through those gates with all his traps, but there's one thing he must always leave behind, his heart.

When you read or reread the books, I hope you will agree that even if this is Geoffrey Trease's fantasy region, it is a world which has been made vivid and memorable not just by the clarity and loving care of the author's prose, but also by the skilfully executed maps, where every detail of the adventures can be faithfully traced. I can still remember arguing with a class of eleven-year-olds about the exact place where Miss Florey meets Sir Alfred with a spade, and getting them to mark on their own neatly drawn map copies just precisely where they thought the skeletons of the monks would lie.

Let us leave Bannermere with a quotation that sums up Bill and Penny's love for the Cumbrian landscape and also gives a strong hint of their growing feelings for each other.

Spring was really here now. Creamy blossoms gleamed against pink sandstone barns, and in one orchard the long grass was spiky with hundreds of daffodils. I leant across and touched Penny's wrist. 'Look,' I said. She was just in time to see the warm flash of gold before it vanished behind us.

'Oh, lovely!' she said with a little gasp. I had known she would like it.

WINDERMERE

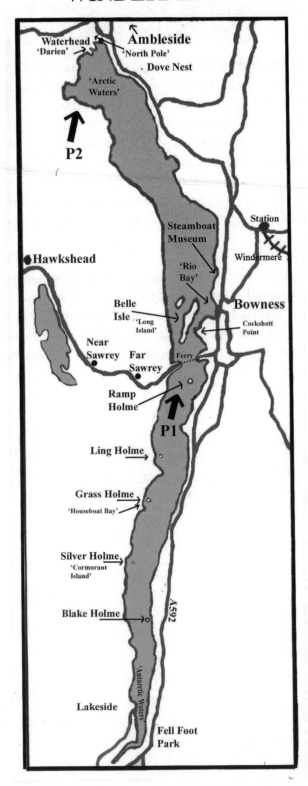

Waterhead
'Darien'

Ambleside

'North Pole'

Dove Nest

'Arctic Waters'

P2

Station

Steamboat Museum

Windermere

Hawkshead

'Rio Bay'

Belle Isle

'Long Island'

Bowness

Cockshott Point

Near Sawrey

Far Sawrey

Ferry

Ramp Holme

P1

Ling Holme

Grass Holme

'Houseboat Bay'

Silver Holme

'Cormorant Island'

A592

Blake Holme

Lakeside

'Antarctic Waters'

Fell Foot Park

46

CHAPTER IV

ROLLING DOWN TO RIO—ARTHUR RANSOME COUNTRY

Windermere, Bowness, Ambleside, Coniston

At ten and a half miles long, Windermere is the longest lake in England and is Cumbria's most popular destination. The town of Windermere was originally a tiny village called Birthwaite until the coming of the railway in 1847, when the company renamed the village after the lake. There then followed a period of building large and luxurious mansions in both Windermere and Bowness, and along the shores of the lake. Wealthy businessmen from the principal towns of Lancashire could either spend their holidays there or even use the railway to commute to work each day.

Those halcyon days for a few rich individuals have long gone. Tourism has become king. The two towns now feel like extensions of each other and it should come as no surprise to learn that Bowness, ideally placed on the middle of the eastern shore, is the most visited town in the whole region. Many of the grand houses have become hotels, and the small harbour throbs with activity throughout the summer months.

Lake Coniston at five miles long is smaller and quieter, though still the third largest of the Lake District lakes. Brooding above everything on the west side of the lake are the slopes of the Old Man of Coniston and its sister peak of Wetherlam.

The literary associations in this heartland of the southern lakes have long been established. Grasmere means Wordsworth; and, to a lesser degree, Coniston is famous for John Ruskin. In the world of Lakeland children's books, the big names are Arthur Ransome and Beatrix Potter. Indeed, so well known are these authors that they have become an important part of the tourist industry. In the next chapter, we shall see that many other stories have settings in these popular surroundings; but first for a while we too must pay homage to the Ransome phenomenon.

There are five full Lake District books by Arthur Ransome, and a fragment of a sixth turned up amongst his papers after his death.

***Swallows and Amazons* (34)**, published in 1930, is the story of the holiday exploration and adventures of the four Walker children, John, Susan, Titty and Roger, on a large lake in the north of England. Steady, reliable and responsible, John, aged about twelve, is the captain of the sailing boat *Swallow*. Mate of the ship, and generally worrying happily about their domestic arrangements, is the slightly younger Susan. The sensitive and imaginative Able Seaman Titty is probably around nine, while Roger, the Ship's Boy, is seven. For a while the story simply details their day-to-day life camping on a near-perfect little island. The narrative is then enlivened by encounters with Nancy and Peggy Blackett, aged respectively thirteen and twelve, who have adopted the role of Amazon pirates. Their Uncle Jim, a sometimes kindly and sometimes irascible middle-aged man who has explored the world and finally settled down to write his memoirs, plays a significant part in the story. It is a narrative which, amongst many other things, involves explorations, unfortunate misunderstandings, a mock war, false accusations, a midnight robbery and the finding of an unusual treasure.

The first sequel, *Swallowdale* (35), published in 1931, mostly takes place ashore on the hills above the lake in a special little valley, while the Walker children wait for their boat to be repaired. Meanwhile, Nancy and Peggy, the Amazon pirates, are being kept at home by the orders of their great-aunt. A real shipwreck, camping life, hound trails, holiday tasks, the demands of adults, a dramatic hill mist and an unlucky accident all vie with each other to claim the reader's attention. Together the friends and allies finally manage to climb the local mountain that they have named Kanchenjunga.

Winter Holiday (36), published in 1933, introduces Dick and Dorothea Callum and returns to the same Lakeland scenes during the depths of a severe winter. As the mighty lake freezes, the new characters are gradually integrated into comradeship with the core group of the original six children. Time is spent on the snowy fells, on perilous cliffs, in a damp igloo and aboard the frozen-in houseboat. Nancy catches mumps but still manages to get her Uncle Jim to prepare a very extraordinary North Pole to receive a special expedition to the head of the lake.

Prospecting, mining and smelting are at the centre of *Pigeon Post* (37), published in 1936, and most of the action is up on the high fells in the midst of a long summer

High up on the slopes of Wetherlam, the explorers get their first cup of water from Titty's Well (illustration by Arthur Ransome).

drought. There are long journeys up nearly empty rivers, dusty treks along baking hot roads and climbs towards the upper fells through parched land. A well is dug, a mine is found, an enemy is harassed and an unreliable pigeon carries the vital message that could save the countryside from an all-consuming fire.

The Picts and the Martyrs (38), published in 1943, features just Nancy, Peggy, Dick and Dorothea. However, most of the story is dominated by the formidable Great-Aunt, who appears to have thrown her gloomy shadow over the entire holidays. A fuller account of this book appears later in this chapter as I reveal how my reading of this last Lakeland story coloured my view of the characters and the events in the first four books.

The purpose of this book is to try and cover all of the children's stories set in the Lake District and Cumbria. In one short chapter, I can't hope to do full justice to one of its two most famous children's writers. To a certain extent I must now turn you over to the specialists. Clare Kendall-Price has provided a book of walks *In the Footsteps of Swallows and Amazons* that offers you the practical guidance you need to follow the author round the familiar scenes. The work of Roger Wardale in *In Search of Swallows and Amazons* and of Christina Hardyment in the recently reissued *Arthur Ransome and Captain Flint's Trunk* will provide you with richly rewarding investigations and thoughtful evaluations of all the details that go into making up Ransome country. In the light of so much expertise, what I am offering are my own personal experiences of reading the books and visiting some of the places.

My father was a ship's officer, serving with the Lamport and Holt line out of Liverpool. He had been to the real Rio and he had even travelled up the real Amazon River to Manaos and Iquitos. None of his three sons followed him away to sea. We did follow him by being voracious readers. When my brothers and I devoured the works of Percy F Westerman, particularly his accounts of voyages under sail in ships' open lifeboats, Dad always enjoyed pointing out where the author had strayed over the line from the real world into make-believe. When I brought home a copy of Ransome's *We Didn't Mean to Go to Sea* and suggested that he read it after I had finished, he gamely agreed.

By the time he had completed the volume about the Walker children crossing the North Sea and ending up in Flushing, he was nodding in agreement and saying: 'It's unlikely but all perfectly plausible.' This was what I had been waiting for and I pressed home my advantage. With the help of my mother, I persuaded him to take our annual summer holiday in Bowness, so that I could see whether I could find any of the places in the Lake District books. So, not without some qualms of conscience, I turned my family into those most despised of Ransome creatures—the holiday trippers. At least my father had been a genuine salt-water sailor, and he had ensured that his sons gained some sketchy theoretical knowledge about sailing by reading the works of prolific Percy.

We travelled, like the Swallows and the D's before us, by the railway line into Windermere Station. There was a direct steam train from Liverpool in those days. You can find the best descriptions of the latter stages of such a journey in *Pigeon Post*, but I was so full of eager impatience to get to our destination that I did not suspect that Oxenholme was the model for Strickland Junction, where the pigeon is released by Roger and Titty.

There is something refreshingly final about the arrival in Windermere Station. It's a terminus. You can't go any further without running into the buffers.

To enter Ransome country at all, you must stop and switch your outlook. As you stand on the platform it's still possible to imagine the Amazon pirates in *The Picts and the Martyrs* trying to adjust between their two worlds in their greeting of Dick and Dorothea.

      'Scarabs, ahoy!' cried Nancy.
      'Hullo!' called Dorothea.
      And then, it was as if Nancy had suddenly remembered something she

had forgotten. She became a different Nancy.

'We are delighted to see you. I do hope you had a pleasant journey.'

… Nancy laughed. Nobody could keep up that sort of thing for more than a sentence or two.

We carried the suitcases outside and caught the bus down the hill to Bowness. I would rather have travelled in Rattletrap, the Blacketts' car, and caught a glimpse of Colonel Jolys as Roger and Titty do in *Pigeon Post*. It would have been fun to be abandoned on a pier as a small boat hove into sight in Rio Bay. At the time it was enough to realise, as the single-decker bus set off along the Lake Road, that I really was, to quote the title of a Westerman book, 'rolling down to Rio' at last.

 Whether you travel by train, coach or car, it is still possible to visit Windermere Station. The remains of the buildings have been taken over by other enterprises and the once rather impressive edifice is now more akin to a wayside halt. The last time I was there, I sneaked on to the platform and took a photograph of the line disappearing back into the world of normality and, I suppose, back to the land of my youth.

Step outside Windermere Station and you can still easily catch a bus, or you can call into the nearby information centre. More excitingly, you can find the clearly signposted trail to Orrest Head. A tame walk to the summit gives you the first chance to see the lake as a whole and pick out some of the features so well known from the endpapers of *Swallows and Amazons*. It's a good way to begin the exploration of the probable Ransome territory.

The fictional town of Rio (whose real-life counterpart is Bowness) is usually treated with disdain by the child characters in Ransome's books. However, I have always liked the place in spite of its crowds, its over-commercialisation and its traffic. The week I spent there with my parents was a happy one. I have been back several times and the positive feeling persists. I think I must be a natural tripper.

On the first evening, I went down to the steamer pier and stared out at the bay. I began to run through the stories in my mind. Just when had the Swallows, Amazons and D's come into this imagined replica of the port in Brazil? I hope my memories will prompt you to stand in the same places and let the relevant parts of the plots unreel before your eyes once more. In *Swallows and Amazons*, the first visit to Rio comes when John, Susan, Titty and Roger go in pursuit of the *Amazon*, after the Blackett girls have just set off a firework on the houseboat's roof. The bay is crowded with boats, and they have to watch out for one of the big steamers. I wonder which it was—*Swan*, *Tern*, or *Teal*, all still sailing the lake today? Roger spots the white sail of the enemy in the waters to the north. A fruitless chase follows, and Susan says that the *Swallow* must call back at the town for supplies. Titty suggests that she be put ashore on a small islet

The *Tern* arrives at the steamer pier in Bowness Bay.

to keep watch, so that the red-capped pirates do not double back to the island landing place and claim possession of the Swallows' tents. That August evening was when I first played the game of choosing which islet would be the best one for Titty's landing place. Close to where I was standing, as I pursued my 'wild surmise', would be the landing stage where Roger sits on guard as the Captain and the Mate of *Swallow* go ashore to purchase some grog (ginger beer) and twenty yards of rope for the lighthouse tree.

Back out in the bay, they picnic on Titty's sentinel island with bread and butter and pemmican (corned beef) and apples. The very mundane nature of their food made the whole world of the books feel accessible.

As the sun dipped below the hills opposite, I suddenly remembered the *Swallow*'s second traverse of the bay at Bowness. It is the morning after the abortive attack on the boathouse on the Amazon River. They have had a tense voyage tacking southwards in the black of the night, where John and his crew of Susan and Roger very nearly became the 'duffers' that their father had warned about. The rest of the night is spent tied to a post on a landing stage. In the morning they see a new Rio which is deserted in a way they had never seen it before. Not a soul is stirring as they set off hurriedly southwards to get back to Titty and to Wild Cat Island. I must admit to a feeling of regret that their voyage takes them home to success. I always favoured the Amazons and hoped they would win the war to become the flagship.

However, I like John better when I think of the voyage to Rio Bay in *Swallowdale*. His misjudgement leads to *Swallow* running into Pike Rock and sinking to the bottom near Horseshoe Cove. The most poignant Ransome simile of all conveys totally how all the children's plans for the holiday are ruined: 'It was as if the summer itself had been the cargo of the little ship and had gone with her to the bottom of the lake.'

Rescued from the deep by John's own determined salvage, patched up by the sympathetic and practical Captain Flint, *Swallow* is brought to the boatyards at the southern end of Rio Bay under jury rig.

The emotional heart of *Swallows and Amazons* is the moment when the real world is thrown into violent collision with the explorers' world, so carefully built up in the mind of John and the others. It is the occasion when Captain Flint calls John a liar. No matter how much he later regrets this outburst and apologises, the adult does not recapture the lost ground until the moment in *Swallowdale* when he superintends and pays for the rebuild of the little ship. In a way, it isn't so much the replacement of the plank and the shaping of the new mast, but the philosophy he can offer her captain, that is the greatest help he gives John:

> 'Don't you worry about it overmuch. When a thing's done, it's done, and if it's not done right, do it differently next time. Worrying never made a sailor.'

Left: Roger on guard in Bowness (Rio) Bay
Right: The injured *Swallow* makes her way to the boatyards in Rio for repairs.
(illustrations by Arthur Ransome)

'It isn't worrying,' said John. 'It's just that I hate myself for being such a duffer.'

'Um,' said Captain Flint, 'I wouldn't mind betting you've been just as much of a duffer lots of times before when nothing's happened. We're all duffers sometimes, but it's only now and then that we get found out.'

The wreck of *Swallow* is like a belated punishment for the risky night sailing episode in *Swallows and Amazons*. It certainly makes John at once more fallible and more likeable.

The repairs to *Swallow* in the boatyards that used to dominate the waterfront to the south of Bowness Bay should remind us that this is also the birthplace of *Scarab*, which is launched in *The Picts and the Martyrs*. Dick's struggle to cope with the tiller, the red sail, and the impatience of men in passing rowing boats, takes place between the shore and the mass of Belle Isle (Long Island in the books). You will not require much imagination to conjure up this confused scenario today.

It was only by closing my eyes that I could hope to 'see' this place in winter. In *Winter Holiday*, Rio becomes an Eskimo settlement and the entire stretch of water in

See the point marked P1 on the Windermere map (p46). Ramp Holme Island, Ferry Nab, Belle Isle and Bowness Bay from the south (photographer: Peter Lewis)

the bay, like the water in the whole lake, freezes solid. Two Bowness episodes in this arctic story stand out—one is where Dick and Dorothea stop to purchase a meat pie on their mistaken quest to overtake the others heading for the North Pole. The other comes earlier, when Captain Flint sets out from the houseboat, tows his sledge on to the ice, heads for Rio Bay and then disappears. Roger cheerfully suggests that he must have gone through a hole in the ice. Later Peggy and the Swallows see him again coming down from the settlement, pulling his sledge behind him, now with an enormous packing-case on it. As Peggy says: 'It only spoils things to be too beastly clever.' They all know it must be something to do with the North Pole, but to maintain their imaginary world they must not ask awkward questions, and 'when it was necessary the explorers looked the other way'.

It is advice that present-day visitors to the real lake must hold on to at all costs. On a busy day up to 100, 000 people can be on or around the water. In such circumstances, it is hard to drive out reality and hang on to fictional companions. I, too, wanted a trip to both the Arctic and the Antarctic of the books. It would take careful management of my parents to see either place.

The first morning of our stay in Bowness, we took the short walk to Cockshott Point so that I could attempt to find Darien and see the island. There was an island there all right—it seemed the right distance away from the shore to match Ransome's map. I had found from an Ordnance Survey map that it was called Ramp Holme. Could it be Wild Cat Island?

The popular promontory of Cockshott Point is too low to be the model for Darien. To gaze over the 'southern ocean' of the lake, it is better to climb Biskey Howe. Take Helm Road out of Bowness, go past the Windermere Hydro and follow the well-signposted and gentle footpath to the top of the outcrop.

There has been much speculation about Ransome's Darien. A visit by steamer to Waterhead takes you close to the entrance of the River Rothay into Windermere. Two peninsulas jut out into the lake towards the south east, but, whilst their cliffs are promising and the whole of Windermere stretches away to the south, there is no island in the appropriate place. My recommendation is that you wait until your visit to Keswick and Derwentwater. Then, as you stand on Friar's Crag, a favourite candidate, you can look out and see St Herbert's Isle and transform it into your own Wild Cat Island.

Nowadays, the Steamboat Museum at Rayrigg Road would claim my attention. Here, you can examine the *Esperance* and realise that it is the model for Captain Flint's houseboat. Even more wonderfully, the museum has two of the dinghies Ransome used as models for boats described in his books. *Amazon* is land-based as she is in too fragile a condition to be sailed. *Coch-y-Bonddhu* (*Scarab*) has been restored through the generosity

See the point marked P2 on the Windermere map (p46)—Waterhead and Ambleside.
Red Screes is the peak in the distance. The mouth of the river and the two possible
Dariens can be seen to the left (photographer: Peter Lewis).

of The Arthur Ransome Society. Swallows and Amazons exhibitions are regular
features of the museum and this fascinating place is now a must for all the books'
devotees.

A steamer cruise to Lakeside and back will take you past more islands and
more points of interest on the shoreline. Blake Holme Island can suggest the
woody ruggedness that one expects of Wild Cat Island near the Lighthouse Tree.
Silver Holme Island, just the right distance away, is the acknowledged inspiration
for Cormorant Island and the place where the treasure was finally found. You
simply have to look closely and imagine it without all those trees. Heading
northwards, it is even more difficult to spot the tiny bay on the west shore which
might do for Horseshoe Cove. It is just south of the rugged island of Grass Holme,
but your steamer will be moving so rapidly that identifying it amongst all those
trees will take skill indeed.

Ramp Holme cannot be the model for Wild Cat Island. It was only because I was
deceived by the size of the lake and the limited view from the shore that I made this

error. It is nowhere near the right size or shape to suit Ransome's maps; but, on the other hand, the more southerly situated Blake Holme has the required size, with room for at least two tents to be hidden amongst its luxuriant trees, and also its nearness to Cormorant (Silver Holme) Island to advance its cause. Ransome himself apparently admitted that it had a serious claim. However, it is Peel Island on Coniston that has the harbour ready and waiting for all who want to land in the right place, using the special marks to guide them in. The 1984 film *Swallows and Amazons* skilfully switches between the two stretches of water and I note that it is the *Tern* which sets the little *Swallow* bucketing dangerously in its wash.

On the day after our great exploration, we conquered the lake to the north in a more leisurely fashion. A journey on board the *Teal* to Ambleside allowed me to sit amongst a huge host of trippers, shut myself off in my own little world and recreate again some of the voyages of the three little boats. You can do this too. I stared at the western shore and became a passenger in the rejuvenated *Swallow* after her repairs in Rio, which allow her gradually to overtake the *Amazon* in the great race at the end of *Swallowdale*. I marvelled again that John, after his disaster at Pike Rock, had the daring to throw his and Susan's weight on the lee side and so lift her keel over the shallows to gain the crucial advantage. Again I mourned for the failure of the Amazons to come out on top.

Next, I tried to imagine an impenetrable mist over the water and the four elders creeping down the lake to their failed rendezvous with Titty and Roger at Swallowdale. Eventually the hordes of fellow travellers broke through into my reverie, and my careful reconstruction vanished amidst the hubbub of conversation.

Disembarking at Waterhead allows you to sample a few genuine Ransome experiences. From the steamboat landing, you must remember to look across the water to see if those south-eastward jutting possible-Darien promontories come up to the standard of your imaginary landscape.

A walk in Borrans Park gives you the chance to search for your preferred site of the North Pole. Apart from the last part of the night of the polar expedition (which is done by sledge and ice-skates), it is curious to report that neither the Swallows nor the Amazons ever actually sail into the extreme north (or indeed the extreme south) in the glimpses that Ransome allows us of their adventures.

Strange as it may seem, it is worth remembering that these polar Windermere waters belong more to Dick and Dorothea, for the Callums are the first to the North Pole in *Winter Holiday*, and, on their maiden voyage in *Scarab* in *The Picts and the Martyrs*, they sail into the river at the top of the lake: 'We needn't go near the steamer pier,' said Dick. 'There's a river on the map.'

A stroll in Rothay Park offers you the opportunity to stand close to that river and imagine the landing of the crew of the little dinghy as they cling to the branches of the bushes until Dorothea scrambles ashore to stamp

Left: Dick and Dorothea have problems on their first sail in *Scarab*.
Right: Nancy reaches the North Pole.
(illustrations by Arthur Ransome)

the anchor into the ground. You can find Rothay Bridge where she crosses the river when she walks into Ambleside in order to buy a cookery book. It is a journey you can easily undertake yourself, though I hope it's unlikely that you will make yourself sick gutting, skinning and cooking your own rabbit when you get home.

Books may have been the inspiration for my visit but I had chosen only one book to take with me on the holiday. It was the last of the Lake District stories—*The Picts and the Martyrs*. Strangely enough, it was the first one I had ever read, but it was the last one I chose to reread.

What a surprise and a revelation it became as I held on to the purple dustjacket and dived deeper into the pages! It was this book which had always made me favour the Amazons and especially Captain Nancy. It was also this book that convinced me that Arthur Ransome's work wasn't just for children but also for discerning adults.

With the possible exceptions of the fantastical *Peter Duck* and *Missee Lee*, I have never since had any fears about returning in later years to my favourite early childhood reading. *The Picts and the Martyrs* is about the world of the adults as much as it is about children, and Nancy isn't just on the bridge of the *Amazon* as usual; she *is* the other sort of bridge, the one that leads you safely from childhood into the adult world. The problem that the author faces her with is satisfyingly complex.

From out of the blue, Nancy suddenly finds that she has to reconcile many conflicting points of view. Dick and Dorothea have been invited to stay at Beckfoot whilst Uncle Jim takes Mrs Blackett on a convalescent cruise round Norway. Great-Aunt Maria is furious to find out that Nancy and Peggy are to be alone in the house with just the cook to look after them, and she sends a telegram announcing her imminent arrival. Nancy knows that the Great-Aunt will be doubly angered if she finds guests have been invited to stay whilst the owner of the house is absent. She also knows that her mother will be upset if the Callums are unable to stay at Beckfoot after all. She believes that Dick and Dorothea are entitled to a holiday where he can get on with his assay work with Timothy and the two of them can learn how to sail the newly built *Scarab*.

Nancy's instincts are to roar defiance at the Great-Aunt, rush off and 'take to the hills', as Peggy suggests. But she is not the 'Ruth'-less person that she aspires to be in her wildest moments. 'Ruth' means compassion or mercy, and the person who would suffer from the wildest of actions would be her mother, who, having been brought up by the Great-Aunt, still lives under an emotionally draining cloud when facing the old lady's disapproval. Any recovery for Mrs Blackett from her exhausting bout of flu would be seriously marred if Nancy misbehaved. It takes a great deal of moral courage for Nancy to fix upon the course of action that she does. To carry it off, when she is surrounded by adults who are at best (like the Doctor) unwilling to help, or at worst foolishly timid or socially inept (like the wretched Timothy Stedding), is a remarkable achievement. In her way, she shows a form of resolution that outdoes that of John as the Swallows are swept out to sea in *We Didn't Mean to Go to Sea* or Dorothea in *The Big Six* when the Death and Glories are covered in a pall of suspicion.

In fact it is Dorothea, the character who so often stands outside the events and views them almost with the eyes of the reader, who recognises the thankless and strange path that Nancy is treading. But it is to the reader alone that Ransome confides the innermost thoughts of the Great-Aunt, which reveal a delicious irony of the book—that Great-Aunt and Great-Niece are remarkably similar in their character and determination. Whilst one strives for control and conformity, the other is working just as hard for freedom and happiness. *The Picts and the Martyrs* is a book about the different ways in which people choose to accept and exercise responsibility. Nancy selects her way deliberately and deserves to succeed. It could be argued that, in spite of Susan's maternal fussiness and the occasional acute maturity of Dorothea's observations, of all the children in the series Nancy is the first to grow up. She still, however, wants to preserve the world she has partly left behind, for the others.

Ransome's contrivance that the Great-Aunt should end up in Dick and Dorothea's *Scarab* and come close to the secret life of the Picts on the very day of her departure is the mark of a master plot-builder. The Great-Aunt's confrontation with Colonel Jolys and thus her forgetting to ask the vital questions of her rescuers is totally in character. Nancy and Peggy get the luck that their sacrifice deserves.

On our final day I asked my parents if we could go to Ambleside once more and try to climb Wansfell Pike. That way I could take a photo that looked down the whole length of Windermere. As the *Tern* chugged north to Waterside, I gazed to the western shore once more and tried to imagine the woods echoing to Colonel Jolys's hunting horns, and the red sail of *Scarab* slipping along with its strange cargo of Great-Aunt Maria Turner.

The old lady's farewell letter, in which she praises the 'notable improvement in both Ruth and Margaret' and comments on Ruth's 'tact', is a fitting reward for Nancy's schemes and stratagems.

'An awful ten days, but worth it to save Mother.'

It isn't just her mother. If John risked the whole of an earlier summer by wrecking *Swallow*, Nancy can truly have been said to have saved this later one by her newly found grasp of the adult world. As she tells Dick, Dorothea and Timothy, the Swallows are coming: 'and [there are] five whole weeks of the summer still to go'.

My time was up but I now knew why, after reading this book as though it were the first in the series, I had always rooted for the heroic Nancy and favoured the Amazons in all of the races.

When I return to Windermere, I always have a strange feeling that it is both a highly convenient and yet a highly unsatisfactory lake for visitors in search of Arthur Ransome's stories. The shape of the lake (if made a little broader in the beam) matches very well those endpapers which become so familiar to his devoted readers. There are islands in all the right places and there are fast-moving and frequent boats to take you past them. Yet of the shore-based locations, only the railway station, Bowness Harbour and some parts of Waterhead can make you feel you are in the true Ransome country.

Coniston Water offers some quieter and more intimate possibilities. Again, however, you are forced to choose just how close you want to get to some of the special places in the books. Ransome's stories now have a very public presence on the tourist trail.

You must find your own balance between seeing the essential locations and trying for an experience that matches those of the children in the stories. The ideal guide is Roger Wardale's *In Search of Swallows and Amazons*, in which he presents his conclusions from forty years of investigations about precisely where the stories are set. Alongside his account of the locations, he develops a fascinating picture of Ransome's own life and the creation of this most famous series of books. Armed with an Ordnance Survey Map and Roger Wardale's book, you will be able to follow many trails to a worthwhile conclusion. In fact, with all its many maps, sketches and photographs you will even be able to sit at home and consider just how true they are to the pictures that Ransome developed in your mind as you first turned the pages.

Here are just some of my own suggestions for explorations:

The road which runs along the eastern side of Coniston takes you near many of the essential Ransome sites. Most important of all, the small parking spaces towards the southern end of the lake allow you the chance to look across to Peel Island with its hidden harbour. A short walk across

National Trust land close to High Peel Near allows you access to the waterside. From here the island stands out clearly, looking as an island should. This is in contrast to the view from the more popular parking site on the A5084 on the western side of the lake, for seen from that point the model for Wild Cat Island merely merges into the background as another clump of the forest. Continue your drive up the road on the eastern side of the lake and you will pass Rigg Wood where Roger Wardale found the remains of a possible igloo (*Winter Holiday*). Halfway up the lake, near The Heald, one of Ransome's Lake District homes, Wardale's book can guide you to the model for 'The Dogs' Home' which plays such an important part in *The Picts and the Martyrs*.

Continue the drive round the head of the lake and make for the main piers, which serve the village of Coniston itself. At the Coniston Boating Centre, you can hire a motor boat or a rowing boat for your own private voyage of discovery. Perhaps you might even penetrate to the extreme foot of the lake and, entering the River Craik, find yourself drifting amongst the reeds of Octopus Lagoon (Allen Tarn).

Or, you can allow the Ransome industry to take over for a while—for there is even a Coniston lake journey which advertises itself as an 'interactive cruise locating the real places' in the Swallows and Amazons stories. The Coniston Ferry Service and Launch proclaim: 'On Coniston Water we will see Beckfoot, Holly Howe, Kanchenjunga, Wild Cat Island, the Amazons' boathouse, and a host of other spots that Ransome used to create his fascinating world.'

The trip is by solar-electric launch, and cruises are normally arranged on Tuesdays from late March to late October, with extra Thursday sailings during school holidays and half-terms. The steam yacht *Gondola* plies the same waters under the aegis of the National Trust, its distinctive shape also perhaps evoking visions of the houseboat.

The list of potential lake views reminds me of an advertisement on the Coniston website which tells you that if you book early enough, you can stay at Bank Ground on the eastern shore and so be at the place whose farmhouse features prominently in the first story as 'Holly Howe'. The proprietors also remind you that the farmhouse and grounds, as well as various other features, were used in the film of *Swallows and Amazons*, starring Virginia McKenna and Ronald Fraser.

Having driven round the lake or ventured forth on to its waters, it is time to consider covering some ground on foot. There are many guide books and leaflets which will tell you how to get to the top of Coniston Old Man (the Kanchenjunga of the books). Again Roger Wardale's meticulous book will tell you how to come closest to the route taken by Nancy and the others in *Swallowdale*. It is on the slopes of Wetherlam that you will find the terrain that Ransome used for High Topps in *Pigeon Post*. You will not be surprised to learn that Mr Wardale has all the necessary information about the mine and Slater Bob, and succeeds in untangling the intricate way in which Ransome entwined the different aspects of the countryside until they fitted his Carnegie Medal-winning adventure.

Another drive is needed to get to the starting place for a piece of real exploration.

You will not quite be going into uncharted territory, for you will certainly need an Ordnance Survey Map (English Lakes—South Western Area) to make the most of your chances of finding the setting for *Swallowdale*. This time a journey down the western side of the lake via the A5084 brings you to the small car park which is located not far south of Peel Island. Your destination lies back across the road on the rising slopes that lead to the Blawith fells. It is called Beacon Tarn on the map, but many Ransome fans believe that it is the model for Trout Tarn in *Swallowdale*. Somewhere between Coniston Water and Beacon Tarn flow the becks that could be the ones forming the falls at either end of the most perfect little valley in all of Ransome's tales. If you want to hunt for it, you must go well prepared, for you will certainly

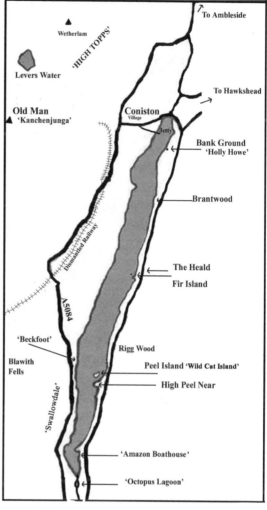

Coniston

find steep rocky slopes, thick bracken and boggy ground. Roger Wardale's advice is to stick as close to the beck as possible. First, however, you must choose the right beck! As always, I recommend that you purchase his book and take the hints dropped by this master detective as he describes his own journey.

For the best of reasons there are many readers of all generations who want to get close to where most of the action of the books took place. In certain seasons of the year I fear there is now a danger of these favourite places being 'loved to death'. I believe that it is high time that we offered some alternative places for a literary pilgrimage. My hope is that the next chapter will give you the chance of looking at the same area from the perspective of several other interesting and enjoyable children's stories about Windermere, Coniston and the countryside that lies around these lakes.

WINDERMERE, CONISTON AND GRASMERE

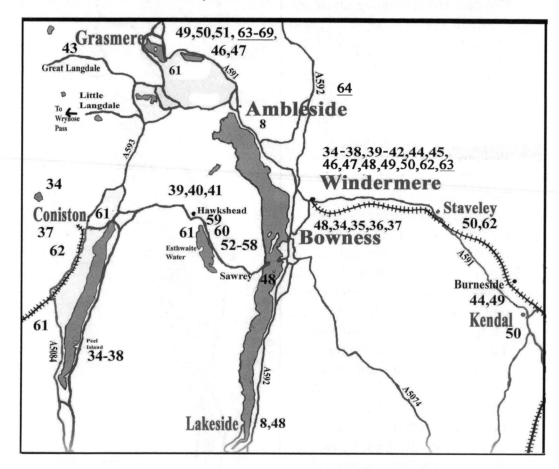

CHAPTER V

NORTH TO THE 'OTHER' COUNTRY

Windermere, Bowness, Lakeside, Langdale, Tarn Howes,
Sawrey, Grasmere, Hawkshead, Coniston

Most of the previous chapter took as its focus the adventures of the Swallows and Amazons on Windermere. You may be surprised to learn that we are not finished with the great lake yet, as there are several more stories you can get to know whilst we make our way through what has often been regarded as exclusively Ransome country. A brief exploration of the Langdale Valleys, which stretch their fingers into the central fells, is also essential, and it is impossible to leave this particular region without some mention of its most famous children's writer—Beatrix Potter.

We start with another family story that is set in a real place. Nowadays the owners of High Arnside Farm not far from Hawkshead make this claim in their advertisement for the two cottages on their land:

> The 'Fell Farm' books by Marjorie Lloyd are based on High Arnside Farm and copies of the three books are available for loan for guests to read during their stay.

Four Family Stories

We begin in fact with not three but four books by Marjorie Lloyd. *Fell Farm Holiday* **(39)**, published in 1951, is the first in a trilogy about the Browne family, who spend three long holidays in a very specific part of the Lake District, during three very different seasons of the year.

Without doubt the author has made every effort to make her books appropriate for boys and girls between the ages of nine and thirteen. For a start, she offers a wide range of young protagonists—all within one family. There are five Brownes altogether: two sets of twins—Patrick and Katharine (Pat and Kay), aged fifteen, and Jan and Hyacinth (whose name is never shortened), aged thirteen—and the youngest, Sarah (Sally), aged eight. Pat is the leader who wants everything shipshape, for, like John Walker, he knows that he is destined for the Navy. Hyacinth is the bookish one, reading whenever she gets the chance and working away steadily at writing her own mystery thriller. Hyacinth appears not unlike Dorothea in the Arthur

Ransome books, and one is tempted to say that Jan resembles Dick in his love of bird-watching, except that everything else about Jan is suggestive of vigorous physical activity rather than the character of a budding professor. Kay is the most domesticated of the five children and seems to take particular care of Sally, trying to include her in their activities wherever it is possible.

The Browne parents, like the Walker parents, are conspicuously absent for all three of the storylines. In this case the mother and father are in India and the children are looked after by their Aunt Gretchen in her London flat when they are not at their separate boarding schools. The holidays, therefore, are the only time that all the children of the family get together. They travel to the Lake District alone and are to be looked after by Mr and Mrs Jenks, the tenants of High Tarn Farm, who are presented throughout the series as warm and loving Cumbrian characters.

But, of course, where these stories diverge from the Swallows and Amazons tales is the location for their adventures. Whilst the lakes and islands are the main magic ingredients of the early Ransome books, it is the walks, scrambles and climbs on the fells that are at the core of the Fell Farm books. There are other differences too—perhaps the most marked being the 'reality' of the physical world explored by the Browne family. This is best exemplified by the Old Man of Coniston, the mountain which is called precisely that in these books, whereas the Walkers and the Blacketts must transform it into Kanchenjunga. The maps that line the endpapers of the Ransome tales are marvels of invention, blending features of Coniston with Windermere, and renaming the islands and the towns. The maps in the Fell Farm books are not works of imagination but records of fact. You too can use them to walk in the footsteps of the children and explore the low and high fells.

The series gets off to a good start by the way in which the author uses the novel idea of each of the four eldest in the family taking it in turns to tell the whole story. After Kay has introduced the family, she carefully escorts her readers to the farm itself. The first stretch of the voyage is the well-known train journey into Windermere station. The children get more and more excited as they leave behind Kendal, and soon draw into the next-to-last station at Staveley. This is the signal for them to scramble to get things ready. They each make a guess at the greeting that they will receive from Mr Jenks, and each is proved to be exactly right. The next stage is the exciting journey by lorry alongside Lake Windermere and then the turn into the road that avoids Ambleside and takes them over Skelwith Bridge. Finally there is the climb off the road and up the steep farm track that takes them to the buildings of the low, whitewashed farm. In each of the sequels, this journey is repeated with subtle variations, but every time it captures the excitement the children feel at their return to a holiday destination that means so much to them.

When they arrive at the farm, the narration switches for a while into Jan's control, and very soon the reader is immersed in an afternoon of bird-watching, told from his point of view. It nearly ends with Hyacinth immersed in the waters of Tarn Hows (as it is spelt in the book, though modern spelling favours Tarn Howes) but she is rescued at the last second by Jan grabbing her plaits! The following day, Kay narrates the story of their first big walk, which has exciting consequences when the weather turns misty and they find they have forgotten their compass. And so on for the rest of the book: for, though not entirely without a plot, the story is really constructed in episodes. A lengthy walk down Ennerdale and the long hitch-hike back home occupy several chapters, and this is followed by Pat's suggestion of a high altitude camp during a period of fine weather. Sally is to be left behind, but the four older ones get permission to stay out over several nights on the fells beyond the Langdale Valley. The climax is when they spend a night in their sleeping bags very near the top of Scawfell (again, this is the spelling used in the books) and wake to find that they have to make their way back down in a rainstorm.

There is a different feeling at the start of *Fell Farm for Christmas* (40), the second book in the short series, published in 1954. Last time, the five children in the story were coming back with happiness to a place they knew well but which the reader didn't know at all. Now each boy or girl can join the Brownes as they see again the familiar scenes. Also, this time the whole book is narrated by Hyacinth. The story of the journey is prolonged for two chapters and the reader joins the Brownes even before they step on the train to set off for the north. There is a real suggestion of a promised land glimpsed distantly as the track winds round Morecambe Bay, where 'you usually get the first view of the fells, looking simply wonderful across the great curve of the bay'.

You catch the feeling of frustration as the final section of the rail journey between Oxenholme and Windermere seems to drag on at less than half the speed of the long haul from London. Every little wayside station is recognised and regretted until they finally reach their destination.

After a restful day during which Hyacinth describes how they get to know again all the animals of the farm and visit the neighbours, the Browne family are ready for action. Marjorie Lloyd once again constructs a set of episodes that range from the stimulating and improbable to the exciting and the dangerous. The family's version of a game of hare and hounds is enlivened by another tremendous incident involving Hyacinth's long plaits. Later she finds herself drawn closer to the world of her twin brother Jan, as he looks after a heron that has become trapped by the ice. However, the most plot-led part of the book involves an encounter with some sheep rustlers, which, as the children ignore adults and the police, rather jars with the sane and sober reality of the rest of the story.

This time the climax of the book is definitely a much-awaited blizzard scene in which Jan and Hyacinth go in search of a snow-bunting and find themselves lots of snow. Family morale sinks to an all-time low when quarrels break out during a long period of being snowed in, but revives with the brilliant game that they play in the capacious barn.

The tail-piece to these books always matches the beginning, and once again we see the children going through the ritual of farewell as they store in their minds the views

FELL FARM CAMPERS

Marjorie Lloyd

Puffin Books 3/6

of the mountains and fells that ring the farm, before they set off to catch the early morning train back to London. They know that next time they see it, the countryside will be covered in new growth; they will never again have the stark clarity of this moment. And this proves to be so with *Fell Farm Campers* **(41)**, published in 1960.

Each book in the series has grown progressively longer. In the Puffin editions, *Holiday* has 153 pages, *Christmas* has 174 pages and *Campers* has 232 pages. It is as though Marjorie Lloyd wants to ask a little bit more from her readers as they grow up with her books. Most surprising of all is that for the third and final book in the series she adopts yet another form of narrative, the third person. It seems that, having brought us close to the family by the individually narrated chapters (*Fell Farm Holiday*), then carried us further into specific relationships by Hyacinth's narrative (*Fell Farm for Christmas*), she wants to end by making us stand back and see how the little group of children fits into the larger world of the Lake District.

The motif of camping fits into this atmosphere splendidly. The Brownes are neither totally independent, nor totally reliant on the Jenks family. However, they must cook at least one meal a day for themselves, and look after their camp and their clothes during the bouts of bad weather. They are moving closer to the threshold of more adult life while still remaining children. The idea of this new life is made all the more appropriate because the season is spring. Marjorie Lloyd is completing her view of the Lake District by writing a story that fits into the remaining school holiday of the traditional British three term year.

Jan and Hyacinth have another exciting bird-watching experience involving an island in the middle of Tarn Hows. There are more details concerning cats and kittens and farm dogs and a vivid account of what it is like to go to the Grasmere Hound Trail. Life under canvas is shown to have as many drawbacks as pleasures. However, there is also a new grittiness in the storyline, for not everyone proves as friendly and easy to get on with as in previous adventures. In particular, the author sustains quite a series of unpleasant encounters between the Brownes and two boys who have cycled there to camp from Barrow. These are interwoven between the usual explorations of the hills and the coping with bad weather in a difficult environment.

The series ends with all the loose ends tied up and with harmony restored by a tremendous show of hospitality around a massive camp-fire.

These are warm and positive books, where the children encounter most of the usual perils of extreme weather in the Lake District without ever coming near to real fear or suffering or even doubt about themselves or each other. The countryside, through three seasons, is described meticulously and the locations and the walks through them are all convincingly real. Not least amongst the attractions of the Puffin editions are the delightful and amusing illustrations by the author and by the excellent Shirley Hughes, who also did the wonderful cover design of *Fell Farm Campers*.

Without resorting to the more strenuous expeditions in the books, it is still possible to recapture some of the delight felt by the Browne children by making a visit to Tarn Howes.

This is one of the Lake District's most popular destinations, and you can walk the two miles there from either Hawkshead or Coniston to enjoy the small body of water which is surrounded by spruce and pine trees. It takes about an hour to circle the whole tarn and there are plenty of places for a picnic. Don't be tempted to try Jan and Hyacinth's expedition to the island in search of owls. It is far better to use your imagination and merely visualise their journey by rickety raft and the long, cold and dangerous swim they had to make to get back. Concentrate instead on looking for the rare red squirrels that can still occasionally be seen. Don't forget to allow the time for a slow and gentle return to where you left the car.

Further expeditions in imitation of the Browne family will require much more planning, preparation and proper equipment. Let us take just one

Tarn Howes in the summer (photographer: Peter Lewis)

example. Nowadays the Ordnance Survey Explorer Map OL06 (South Western Area) and OL07 (South Eastern Area) will be essential if you want to make your way via the head of the Greater Langdale Valley to the Brownes' camp near Sprinkling Tarn. Once there, given suitable weather, the descriptions in *Fell Farm Holiday* all begin to fall into place. The Brownes' own earlier confusion in the mists, which ended up with them mistakenly coming down Ennerdale and then having to hitch their way back to Coniston, should always be kept in mind as a warning about how easily danger can overtake you on the high fells.

Being commanded to go to the fells of Westmorland where 'there is still some decent air to breathe' is the starting point of the story called ***The Family at Foxy Beck*** **(42)**, published in 1967. It allows Marjorie Lloyd to give yet another perspective on life in the Lake District. Those who live in the region all their lives have a greatly different attitude to the countryside that surrounds them from those who opt to take their holidays amongst the sheep, the lakes and the fells. There is immediately a contrast between the chores of working life and the pleasures of recreation, as we shall see when we come to consider the realistic ***The Farm in Mallerstang*** **(88)** (see page 122) as against the almost idyllic Fell Farm stories.

The Legge family are translated to a small cottage, Foxy Beck, between Ambleside and Coniston, because of crucial health concerns. Mr Legge has ruined his health and his spirits by dedication to his job as a photographer. An enforced rest in a healthy environment is prescribed by the family doctor. Thus this story is about people who neither belong nor are 'just visiting'.

After an initial night-time rail journey, the reader shares in a whole series of familiarisation experiences as the family explores their new world. First of all there is the cottage itself with its strange bedrooms and staircases and unfamiliar kitchen. Then there are the preparations for their new schools. Getting to know the neighbours is followed by the befriending of various domestic animals which wander into their new domain. As the mother grapples with the problem of providing food and keeping clean in a primitive cottage, the children begin to enjoy their environment.

Gradually, and almost unobtrusively, the family settle in to both their new home and their new schools. All the while, the ailing Mr Legge is watched over as he takes the first tentative steps towards recovering his health and his spirits. That is the entire plot of the book, and it is Marjorie Lloyd's achievement that her tracing of each daily activity holds your attention without resorting to any melodrama or contrivance. The passing of the months is used to give the reader a picture of the Westmorland landscape in many of its different moods. This is blended very effectively with Mr Legge's growing awareness of the potential for marvellous photographs in the landscape around him.

All through the book the children have been wondering just how long their stay in the hills will continue. By the end, even the once-hesitant Alison, who is now looking forward to the prospect of an archaeological dig on the Hardknott Pass, has become a total convert to their new way of life. The winter lies ahead; but when their father decides they can stay at Foxy Beck, the whole family rejoice in the prospects of the future as they watch once more the sun going down behind Wetherlam.

Whilst in the vicinity of the Langdale valleys, it is time to mention *Yan, The Story of a Lakeland Lamb* (43) by Fiona Satow, published in 1975, which is set in Great Langdale on a farm run by Tom and Hannah. 'Yan, Tan, Tethera' are the old Cumberland words for 'One, two, three', and in this book they are the names given to the triplet survivors of an old ewe who has given her last fragile offspring to the world before perishing in a sudden rainstorm. For sixty-four pages the author traces the life cycle of a Herdwick lamb as it faces the challenge of survival in a Lakeland valley. Fiona Satow ends the book with an uncompromising and yet uplifting scene in which Yan plays her own part in the continuing story of the Herdwick sheep.

The threat to little Yan

Offcomers and Outcasts

Now let us look at two very different books which take even younger children via the Ransome route into that Lakeland region which has come to mean so much. *The Offcomers* (44) by Elfrida Vipont, published in 1965, is in the Reindeer series produced by Hamish Hamilton for younger readers. British children living on a farm in the Lake District are having distant American cousins to stay in the period leading up to Christmas. Neither group of children is looking forward to the experience. After treating their guests as 'offcomers' or outsiders for a while, Robert and Jane relax enough to find Betsy and Steve much more fun and much nicer than they could have hoped.

Perhaps the best moment in the book is not the dramatic rescue of an injured climber at the end, but the description of Betsy and Steve's recognition of the marvellous skills of the dog and the shepherd as they bring together a flock of sheep high in the fells. It seems there is something special about this remote place after all.

The Year of the Worm (45) by Ann Pilling, published in 1984, is a book with a much tougher tone but again with a happy ending.

The damaging power of an unfortunate nickname can never be underestimated. Peter Wrigley has been called 'Worm' ever since his primary school teacher talked inadvertently about 'wriggly worms', and the name was immediately applied to the boy who was undersized and weak-looking for his age. It is a trip to the Lake District that is destined to transform his fortunes, and the book is cunningly constructed so that Peter's triumph at the end, brought about by a mixture of determination and good luck, balances out the disaster of the incident at the beginning, where a blend of bad luck and lack of confidence marks him out as an object worthy of contempt and pity. It is an inspirational story about how you should never give up hope.

Daphne and Rachel Explore Brazil's Lakeland

Unlike the other members of the 'Big Four' writers of girls' school stories, Angela Brazil did not write series literature. It is rare for her to use the same set of characters in a second book. *St. Catherine's College* (46), published in 1929, is one of the exceptions, for, as the dustjacket proclaims: 'New readers will enjoy this book as much as those who met Rachel in *At School with Rachel*.'

The book makes an interesting start when Daphne, the first of Rachel's school friends that we meet, is 'hauled over the coals' for breaking the school rules. We soon see that Daphne doesn't go in for minor infringements. Her crime has been to steal her aunts' car and to set off out into the English countryside with Rachel as an unwilling and very frightened passenger.

Daphne, as the readers soon discover, is very good at manipulating the aunts with whom she lives when not at school. And so it is that Rachel gets to spend part of the holidays with Daphne and be invited on a tour of the Lake District in the back of an open-topped car. This time Aunt Mabel is firmly behind the wheel. After making their way from the south of England and through the Midlands, the travellers proceed via Wigan and Preston to Lancaster. 'Presently they were in Westmoreland [the old-fashioned spelling is used], going through Kendal to Bowness, on Lake Windermere.'

They arrive in Windermere at quite a late hour, for they have been delayed by punctures on their journey. However, from the windows of the hotel, by the light of the moon, they can see 'a vista of gleaming silver water and great sombre ranges of mountains behind'.

The next morning the lake has become blue 'in a setting of green woods and purple hills'.

Next they catch a steamer from Bowness to Ambleside and walk back to their hotel along the high road by the lake. The two girls are snapping with their cameras, for there is to be an exhibition when they get back to school. A contrast is drawn between the mass of visitors Rachel and Daphne encounter, and those days when the countryside could be enjoyed in tranquillity, 'when no motor-cycles or charabancs disturbed the roads and a poet could compose his verses in peace, undistracted by the racket of the passing traffic'. One wonders what Angela Brazil would have made of the summer traffic along the road between Ambleside and Bowness nowadays.

The following days of the holiday take in Dove Cottage at Grasmere and then the churchyard where the Wordsworth family is buried.

The River Rothay, which he loved, rushed by within a stone's throw, and as they watched the yellow sunset glow behind the old church and fade away among the eternal hills, they felt there could be no fitter resting-place for him who held all the sights and sounds of nature so dear.

Coniston and Ruskin also get a mention, and then, after a 'hasty run' to Derwentwater and Ullswater, the aunts and their passengers are forced to begin the return journey. Indeed, the Lake District in this book is no more than an interlude in the longer story. The holiday does not drive forward the plot of the story, but it confirms certain vital attributes of Rachel's character, which Angela Brazil wants to make use of in the second half of the book.

At this point it is also worth mentioning Angela Brazil's 1944 book, *The School in the Forest* (47), for its last chapters, involving a trip to the region, repeat the same information about Windermere, Grasmere, Ambleside and Coniston.

Another arrival in Windermere by car is to be found in *Back-Stage* (83), one of the famous Wells series by Lorna Hill, published in 1960. In this story, two of the well-established series characters, Jon and Vicki, take Anna, the nominal heroine of the story, north to their home in Northumberland. They travel via the Lake District as winter closes in on it.

One of the highlights of the journey is when they stop at the rising ground above Bowness:

Below us, a diamond tiara of lights twinkled, and we knew it was the tiny lakeland town of Bowness-on-Windermere. Beyond it, with a pathway of shimmering moonlight splashed across it, lay the lake itself.

Ambleside proves to be full of cars: 'Laden with skis strapped on to their roofs or running-boards or sticking out of their windows, they edged their way along the narrow streets.'

We shall follow their adventures further on page 113 when we too reach Keswick.

By the Sides of Windermere

In its 261 pages the school story *The Mystery Prize* (8) by Helen Kent, published in 1939, has many features that remind you irresistibly of several other Lakeland books. Most notably, as we shall see in a later chapter about Derwentwater (page 107), there is the delivery of a strong religious message which underpins the behaviour of many of the women and girls who are at the centre of the action. However, the main part of the storyline takes place near the banks of Lake Windermere rather than Derwentwater, with, as we have already observed, another vital episode unfolding on the shore of Morecambe Bay (page 13).

Hope Harland, the heroine of the tale, is at a school called Queen's Heightside, and the story also belongs decisively to the genre of the girls' school story. When you consider that the book also has a 'lost in the mountains' episode and a race in the teeth of the rapidly incoming tide, you realise the author has made full use of the possibilities offered by the landscape. The author sets the scene:

> Queen's Heightside lay in a miles-wide natural hollow on the mountain-slope of the fells, high above Lake Windermere … In front of the house was a huge circular sunk lawn, surrounded by a grassy bank. This in turn was surmounted by flower-beds, while another broad stretch of velvet-smooth turf parted off a wide herbaceous border, backed by shrubs. The whole of the front of Heightside formed a great amphitheatre of real beauty. At the bottom, marble steps led to a lily-pond, fed by a gurgling stream from the hills, singing joyously on its way to join the lake far below.

A voyage on a lake steamer takes Hope past the famous Storrs Hall where we learn

Mrs Lodore tells the girls about the mystery prize.

that in 1825 a regatta was held in honour of Sir Walter Scott. Further up the lake, before the steamer pulls in to the jetty at Waterhead over to the east, she is shown Dove's Nest, where Felicia Hemans (who wrote the famous poem 'Casabianca') lived for a time. Later, Ambleside is described as 'the delightful town, where a scrumptious North Country tea was awaiting them'. However, this is not until after the schoolgirls have made the ascent of Wansfell Pike which, after an adventure lost in the mist, begins the process of dedication to God that Hope completes at school that night as she witnesses a glorious sunset over the fells.

To the modern reader the strong emphasis on the intervention of religion into the lives of teenage girls will read rather strangely. Nevertheless there is still quite a lot of pleasure to be gained from imagining the school above Windermere and tracing the real journeys along the lake and through the surrounding countryside.

To the Foot of Windermere

The Deans to the Rescue (48) by Kathleen Fidler, published in 1957, is a book which gives you a full flavour of the lower reaches of the famous lake, including a visit to the celebrated station platform by the steamer pier.

This book is one adventure from the long-running Deans series by Kathleen Fidler. Quite often the Dean children—David, Sally and Bartholomew (always called 'Buffin')—begin the story in their home town of Wigan but end up on holiday in a new and more exciting location where a mystery unfolds. In this story, Buffin and Camille, the French girl from next door, find themselves on a trail which leads them to a small farm at the foot of Lake Windermere. Coincidence plays a big part in making the plot work, but the adventure out on the biggest lake in England makes good use of well-known locations.

The Lake District part of the adventure really begins at Carnforth Station, where the children separate from the supervisory adults in order to cycle their way to the cottage and caravan that are to be their holiday home. Eventually their long, hot journey comes near its completion:

Buffin and Camille spy on the enemy cruiser near Blake Holme (illustration by Reg Forster).

Below them was Lake Windermere—mirroring the blue sky and the dark trees. To the north it widened, and across the lake they could see a timbered dock wall, the roof of a station, an hotel by the waterside and then, rising like waves of green behind it, the forested fells of Furness, the Great Green Hows.

From this point onwards, Lakeside Station, Gummer's How, the road to Bowness, Blake Holme and Ramp Holme islands all have their part to play in the exciting events which start to accelerate towards a terrific climax which has poor Buffin tied and gagged on a speedboat heading northwards, with the villains contemplating tying his legs together and dropping him overboard. Ramp Holme, the Ferry Inn, the Nab, the straits between Belle Isle and the mainland all rush by in the near darkness.

There's a happy ending, of course, and there are many more Dean adventures to come. However, the dashing to and fro amongst those same islands that gave Arthur Ransome part of his inspiration for *Swallows and Amazons* gives this particular Dean outing a certain added piquancy.

On first reading it seems that the little farm based at the foot of Windermere must be entirely fictitious. However, closer examination reveals that certain details must be based on the mansion that once stood on the grounds of what is now the National Trust property at Fell Foot Park. A visit to this substantially restored Victorian park is extremely worthwhile. You can find it just off the A592, the road between Bowness and Newby Bridge. In the spring and early summer, it has magnificent displays of daffodils and rhododendrons, and there are eighteen acres of grounds to explore. Best of all is the lake frontage, the view across to Lakeside and the substantial imitation-Gothic boathouse and tea-room. Little does Buffin know that it is near that same boathouse in the middle of the night that he is to fall into the hands of the ruthless thieves!

The boathouse

Just where is the Beresfords' Home?

Much more elusive in their geographical references are three of the books in the Beresfords series by Peter Lethbridge, already mentioned in Chapter I (see page 6).

Dinah and Roger are the red-headed twins, fun loving, cheeky and impetuous. John is the dominant but friendly elder brother, destined by seniority to make most of the decisions. Pat, also older than the twins, is dark haired, serious and more conscious of their mother's worries about their welfare and safety. Each has a character trait or hobby to delineate him or her in the reader's eyes so that there is no confusion with the rest of the family. John is proud of his physical prowess, enjoying both climbing and boxing. Roger is obsessed by food (a quick nod here should be given to Arthur Ransome's Roger Walker and his liking for chocolate) but also carries a book with him to read if the occasion presents itself. Pat is a painter of some sensitivity and merit. Dinah is the lover of all wildlife, particularly birds, and is the dedicated keeper of a nature diary.

The solving of puzzles, usually involving mysterious strangers, is bread and butter to this sort of family. Most of the zest in the group is provided by Dinah, who will never take no for an answer, and, quite rightly, refuses to be excluded from any adventures by the protectiveness of her brothers.

That Peter Lethbridge was writing about a very real Lake District soon becomes clear in spite of the fact that bogus names are used to obfuscate some of the locations. *The Beresfords in Tarndale* (5) provides us with some of the clearest clues about where the author was envisaging, but as that takes us away from the Beresfords' home territory, you will find it in the earlier chapter about Morecambe Bay (see Chapter I).

The author gives the village in which they have their home the name of Milthwaite. He first lays out his fictional landscape in *Lakeland Adventure* (49), published in 1949. The centre of the Beresfords' world is The Mill Café, which they run with their mother.

> The mill stream was a swift-flowing beck that rose far up among the jagged rocks of the towering mountains which shadowed Milthwaite valley on every side. Below the meadow lay the quiet margins of the mile-long lake …

The Beresfords in *Lakeland Adventure*

As they contemplate reopening the café for the summer season, they take in the scene that surrounds them:

> Crossing the low stone bridge which led over the tumbling beck, they paused
> a moment to watch the boaters rowing round the little island in the centre
> of the lake. The great sheet of water lay blue and tranquil in the morning
> sunshine; and on every side of the valley rose the mountains, great peaks
> of grey and purple.

It is in the dedication of this first book that Peter Lethbridge gives some hints about the real places that inspired the home for his heroic family of children: 'To all my friends at Grasmere, Windermere and Kendal,' he declares. These are the words which suggest that the real location, which stands near a mile-long lake with an island in the middle, could only be one place—the town of Grasmere.

Lakeland Adventure is one of the few stories in this survey which contain scenes that happen in real places in the important Lakeland town of Kendal.

> To get to the ironmongers the boys had to go down several side streets and
> the narrow alleys known as 'Courts', which are numbered, and date from
> the times when the Scots used to make raids on the border country and
> beyond. The 'Courts' were built between the houses to make the fighting
> easier and defence more obstinate; but today they only serve to give
> fascinating glimpses of the castle and the country round the town.

Back in Milthwaite, both the weather and the surrounding scenery play an important part in the rest of the story. Torrential rain causes lake levels to rise, and the idiotic behaviour of a gang of delinquent youths in a rowing boat leads to a dramatic rescue from drowning. The rest of the book is a series of 'cops and robbers'-style adventures, culminating in a car chase on the way to Keswick.

The 1951 story, ***The Boy from London*** **(50)**, is perhaps the most intense of the Beresford stories. This is partly because it does not principally concern the Beresfords themselves until the start of Chapter 9. By then, Peter Lethbridge has ensured that readers will have completely identified themselves with young Jeremy Trent, who has run away from his repulsive and vicious stepfather to seek for the only home he has ever known, a farm to which he was evacuated during the war. Unfortunately, he has only a hazy memory of where he stayed. He fakes his own suicide by leaving his clothes by the side of the Thames and stows away on the back of a wagon. In a separate branch of the narrative, the reader learns that his stepfather, Stan, has seen through Jeremy's plans and is on his trail, hitching up with a travelling fair run by one of his confederates in crime. He, too, is heading north.

The world of the Beresfords, no matter what dangers they run, has basically been shown as a secure one; and that is why Jeremy's plight as a lonely, frightened boy on the run from a malevolent adult is all the more likely, by contrast, to win the sympathy of the reader. In the course of a friendly lift which he gets across the Pennines, we begin to pick up the clues about just where Milthwaite, the Beresfords' home, is meant to be. Jeremy's first arrival point is Kendal, and there he feels that he recognises something about the tall spire of the church in the town. He is even more certain that he knows the level crossing at Staveley, where he once watched the trains on the way to Windermere.

The lorry carrying him presses on.

> They were climbing another hill, and that brief glimpse of the mountains vanished. This time it was a very steep incline, and as they reached the top he saw, far below, a great sheet of water that shimmered like an aquamarine.
>
> A little nearer lay the gray huddle of a town, with great dirty engine sheds and an unlovely railway. That must be Windermere.

A little while later he is found by John, Roger, Pat and Dinah. We are once more in the fictional Milthwaite with the Beresfords. Once again Jeremy (and the reader) learns that the Beresfords live in a house near an old water mill, converted into a café and on a road by the lakeside. Once more the lake is unnamed, but there are boats for hire belonging to the café and there is an island in the centre of the lake. Milthwaite has its pub and its church, and hundreds of holiday visitors. If the illustrations are to be believed, then it also has a market place and its own mercat or market cross.

As they search for Jeremy's aunt and uncle's farm, the Beresfords criss-cross the Lake District and fit in a visit to the Ruskin memorial by the side of Derwentwater (see page 109). As Stan pursues Jeremy, and the Beresfords help their new friend to seek for his home, the book moves to a climactic close at a fairground near Kendal, involving a Romany family who have helped the young boy before.

Danger in the Hills (51), published in 1953, has a much more straightforward theme—that of protecting a very special bird from the

The market cross as shown in *Danger in the Hills* (illustration by Geoffrey Day)

Watching quietly near the secret nest of the eagles (illustration by Geoffrey Day)

attacks of egg-collectors. Peter Lethbridge has Golden Eagles and their nest on a nearby crag to Milthwaite. (Nowadays, it is the ospreys which have come to breed at Bassenthwaite that arouse the public interest and the organised protection.)

The time is the Easter holidays and the birds are in danger not just from rubber-necking sightseers and the local teenage tearaways of the village, but also from the totally unscrupulous attentions of a mad collector. Naturally the Beresfords and Jeremy organise their own resistance to all that menaces the safety of the birds of prey. This allows the author to involve his characters in adventures which include a boxing match, headlong chases and the dramatic rescue of an injured policeman.

From Windermere to Coniston

The scene of the action of our next stories moves for a while to Coniston, though the use of Windermere Station as the gateway to the lakes does not disappear altogether.

But first we must pause, for it is time to consider taking the short journey by ferry across the centre of Lake Windermere in order to set foot on the farms and in the village that are forever associated with the stories of Beatrix Potter. A visit to such a special place can only be enhanced by making a pilgrimage in order to get there.

This entails a walk from the centre of Bowness, round the shores of Windermere, across the lake by the ferry and up over to the fells of Claife Heights, to the village of Sawrey. Here you may see the farmhouse of Hill Top, where Beatrix Potter lived, and which is the setting for fifteen of her books. The walk is categorised as 'easy' and is along well-marked footpaths and roads but can take up to five or six hours. It does involve covering ground which, at times, can be muddy and rough, and there is one stiff climb, which is short but steep. For those less determined or less physically active, there is a shuttle bus and the ferry bus, which can help you make the experience as long or as short as you like. The guidance that you can find in Beatrix Potter World at Bowness makes further details mostly redundant.

Nevertheless, there is something satisfying about walking along by Cockshott Point, before you get to the ferry crossing, and experiencing at first hand a part of the second great gift that Beatrix Potter gave to the nation, for this stretch of land is just one of the many Lakeland treasures (including also the Tarn Howes estate so beloved by the Fell Farm children) that she bequeathed to the National Trust.

So much has already been written about the most famous children's writer associated with the Lake District that the rest of the references here will indeed be brief. The National Trust assures all visitors that the house at Hill Top (purchased over a hundred years ago in 1905) 'remains as she left it' at her death in 1943, and that 'in each room can be found something that appears in one of her books'. Outside, they add, 'the cottage garden contains the same pleasing mix of flowers, herbs, fruit and vegetables as grown by Beatrix'.

I should at this point just mention that although the Derwentwater and Keswick landscapes are covered in a later chapter in this book, the stories which draw upon those backgrounds actually preceded the ones set in and around Hill Top, her final and most beloved workplace and home. The farm at Hill Top and the village of Near Sawrey belong to the second phase of her long association with the Lake District.

Beatrix Potter drew her inspiration for more than fifteen of her stories from the surroundings of Hill Top and the village of Near Sawrey. *The Tale of Ginger & Pickles* (52), published in 1909, was set in the village shop, and the fringes of Esthwaite Water can be discerned in the illustrations for her 1906 book, *The Tale of Mr. Jeremy Fisher* (53). Experts suggest that the lily-pads on Moss Eccles Tarn provided another germ of the idea for that story of the fisherman saved by his unpleasant-tasting mackintosh. The Windermere Steamboat Museum (see page 54) has Beatrix Potter's rowing boat, which she used on this U-shaped stretch of water, amongst its exhibits.

 It is possible to take a comfortable walk to Moss Eccles tarn from Near Sawrey by starting in the lane opposite the Buckle Peat Guest House. After passing through the houses and farm buildings, the lane turns into a track that is signposted 'Bridleway Claife Heights'. There is a farm gate to negotiate, and then a sign for 'Claife Heights/The Tarn', and twenty minutes later you are there at the water's edge.

The Tale of the Pie and the Patty-Pan (54), published in 1905, contains other views of Sawrey including one of the Tower Bank Arms. At the centre of all of this is the farmyard at Hill Top, which is the setting for two stories of 1908. The first, *The Tale of Jemima Puddle-duck* (55), recounts the misadventures of the unlikely heroine, and was published in 1908, as was also *The Tale of Samuel Whiskers or The Roly-Poly Pudding* (56), which explores deep behind the skirting boards and up on to the roof of the same house. Meanwhile *The Tale of Tom Kitten* (57), published in 1907, captures the essence of the house and garden during the period of spring and early summer. *The Tale of Pigling Bland* (58), published in 1913, takes us back to the yard again as Bland and Alexander set off to market. It is interesting that this last tale should once again bring up the thorny subject of local government reorganisation. The two pigs, you will remember, only had licences to go to market in Lancashire. An old map will show you that quite a lot of the territory round Sawrey and Hill Top once belonged to the Red Rose county (Lancashire) but was lost to it by the formation of the administrative district of Cumbria in 1974. At one point the two little pigs see a vision of paradise:

> The sun rose while they were crossing the moor, a dazzle of light over the tops of the hills. The sunshine crept down the slopes into the peaceful green valleys, where little white cottages nestled in gardens and orchards.
> 'That's Westmorland,' said Pig-wig.

Pig-wig is the young female pig that Bland acquires as a companion on his travels after brother Alexander has been taken back home. In the end Bland and Pig-wig make their dramatic escape over Colwith Bridge and go to live in Little Langdale, safe in Westmorland.

We too must continue on our way, following the trail perhaps of Timmy Willie, the visiting country mouse, in *The Tale of Johnny Town-Mouse* **(59)**, published in 1918, as he makes his way by clothes hamper to Hawkshead. Here we can also see that the building that served as a model for Tabitha Twitchit's shop is now the ticket office for the National Trust's Beatrix Potter Gallery. Finally, as we take a long look back on the road that leads onwards from Sawrey, we can strain our eyes for a glimpse of the badger and the fox as they fight their interminable battle in the copses and banks and on the gentle hills that surround us in *The Tale of Mr. Tod* **(60)**, published in 1912.

 A visit to the Beatrix Potter World in Bowness is a useful preliminary—or, if you have younger children, an alternative—to crossing the great lake and attempting to become a part of the daily quota of visitors that is permitted, on a strictly timed basis, on to the sacred sites at Hill Top in Near Sawrey. At the Bowness Old Laundry, twenty-three of Beatrix Potter's tales are brought to life in three-dimensional displays. It is thus possible without effort to 'visit' Jemima Puddle-duck's woodland glade and see whether she escapes from the 'sandy whiskered gentleman'. Mr McGregor's greenhouse, where favourite Potter characters try unsuccessfully to conceal themselves, can be satisfyingly scary for those children with the right amount of imagination. Nowadays, there is also the really easy option of taking a 'virtual walk' through Lakeland to see all the places which inspired the famous author.

Next we turn to *Blue Tarn Mystery* **(61)** by James Shaw, published in 1953, for that puts the focus on an area which overlaps in some ways with the territory of both Ransome and Potter.

Brian and Edna (even their names seem to date them to the 1940s) are on the brink of entering university and have come north for a holiday with their aunt and uncle, who live in a cottage just three miles from Coniston. The story of their interesting encounters with the disguised Miss Fischer, with the irascible and mysterious scientist called Tavernor, and with the lonely orphan Beryl Vernon draws very deeply on the real places that surround the lake and the nearby Old Man. Indeed, the twins first make the acquaintance of Beryl, an attractive girl of near their own age, when she becomes stranded on an islet in the lake. They rescue her boat and carry 'the damsel in distress' to the shore from what is most likely to be Peel Island.

Later excursions, as a mystery develops around them, are taken to the town of Coniston and to the Ruskin Museum itself. Another day sees them setting off on a long round trip by bike to Ambleside, Rydal and Grasmere so that they can visit Dove Cottage. The author then has them travelling down the east side of Windermere until they can reach the ferry to cross and make their return journey alongside Esthwaite Water.

The climb to the Blue Tarn of the title is frustrated several times by different events, and it is not until the final third of the book that the reader learns the secret of the place that has been made deliberately inaccessible. The author contrives both a surprise ending and a dangerous chase on slippery hillsides before everything is resolved and justice is done.

To Prove Yourself a Hero

B Flight (62) by Bruce Carter was published in 1970. Fell-running and flying might seem two subjects that are unlikely ever to be bracketed in the same story, and yet, from this unlikely premise, Bruce Carter (real name Richard Hough) constructs a tale of the First World War which is both very exciting and very moving. The exact locale for the main village in the story is kept very hazy, but one suspects that Coniston or Ambleside may have been amongst the places that inspired the author to create his fictional Amplethwaite. No sooner did I come to this tentative conclusion than those old county borders reared their heads once more. Coniston was in Lancashire, but Amplethwaite is referred to as a Westmorland town. The very real locales of Windermere, Staveley and

Preston railway stations also play significant parts in the action.

Though a major part of the plot is concerned with young Will Sutton's exploits as a pilot in the Royal Flying Corps, the story starts and finishes in the Lake District. It begins, in fact, with a race, the race of Will Sutton as he tries to beat the deadline for late arrivals to the small Amplethwaite Private School in Westmorland. It is a point of honour to arrive at the last minute, cheered on by the girls who are sitting on the wall waiting for the boys to put in their final sprints. Amongst the spectators is Vicky, a girl with cascades of chestnut hair, a lively personality and a beautiful bell-like voice, and Will makes up his mind that he must risk the jibes of his schoolmates and ask if he can walk her home.

At sixteen, Will is as old as the century; and, though the war in France might seem a world away, the thoughts of all the boys are focused on the conflict by the news of the death of the previous year's school captain. Soon they will be old enough to enlist and to be transformed from mere schoolboys into men who must face up to the prospect of imminent death.

Meanwhile, all Will's nerves are keyed up for the momentous prospect of trying to win the affection of Vicky. In the pouring rain at the end of the school day, the two young people discover the new pleasure that they can have in each other's company. It somehow becomes an accepted fact that Will shall enter the Junior Guides race at the coming Amplethwaite sports. It appears that Vicky requires him both to compete and to win as a part of the bargain for her affection.

On the day of the Amplethwaite Races everything goes disastrously wrong even though Will knows he has the speed and the stamina to take first place. A slip on a mountain ghyll sends him crashing to the ground with a searing pain in his left ankle. He forces himself to hobble to the finish but the mortification of failure has a crushing effect on his morale. The rolled-up leather belt which he had given to Vicky for her to hold and to keep for ever if he won is returned to him the next day by her little sister. The note she sends with it is bitingly cruel, for she declares that she had expected too much of a mere schoolboy.

Several weeks later Will rises early in the morning and pedals off secretly to Windermere Station to make his way to London to join the Royal Flying Corps.

> He left behind him the stone walls and fells, the turning bracken, the running
> becks, the winding tracks and lanes of Westmorland; and in his room a pile
> of school books and exercise books, and a half completed model aeroplane.

And, of course, he had left behind 'the lovely Vicky who cared for him no longer'.

When finally he makes it through all his flying training and gains his wings, he feels more ready to face his home town.

His worries about meeting his old friends again prove groundless, for they too are all caught up in the part they are to play in the fighting now they are of age to be volunteers. Vicky is away from home and the mere mention of her is enough to set off his usual mixture of contradictory emotions and memories. However, on the way to London again, his train stops at Staveley and the train from the south pulls in at the opposite platform. As the train moves forward again he sees Vicky in the compartment.

> There were perhaps three seconds when both windows were open and Will and Vicky could look unbelievingly at one another across the gap, and there was time for only one of them to speak. Vicky uttered only two words as they were drawn relentlessly apart amidst the sound of turning wheels and escaping steam. 'Oh, Will!' she called. It was a heart-rending appeal, unmistakably and at once a cry of remorse and love and despair.

The experiences of Will in France are as horrendous and harrowing as any reader of stories about the First World War would expect them to be. The sympathetic understanding of a veteran of the Second World War (Bruce Carter/Richard Hough was himself an RAF Typhoon pilot) for the extraordinary hell that those First World War pilots went through is aptly conveyed in the subsequent fifty pages. Ironically, it is a bullet in Will's foot which means that he will be sent home and that he will never be able to run again. He arrives back at Windermere Station and is ferried home in time for Christmas like a hero in the large taxi. The world of his childhood is still waiting for him there and he looks again at the half-finished model aeroplane. His award of the MC has made him accepted as a hero but he takes a greater satisfaction from being able to hobble out on to the fells and see once more the shepherd bringing home the injured ewe. 'He was at peace in the world he loved.'

Only one thing remains. He is invited to Vicky's parents' on Boxing Day and learns from her mother that, though still absent, she too has been changed by her service in the nursing corps in the field hospitals of France. She will arrive home the next day.

The one quality that the war has given him that he will always be thankful for is the capacity to make a quick decision. Will's mind is now made up. And so the author contrives the happy ending that everyone would want by a delightful scene involving a motor-bike ride on to the platform of Preston Station and a slow return to Amplethwaite, with the passenger on the pillion who is now going to claim forever the leather belt that in this novel is the symbol of total commitment to another person.

A railway journey first brought us to Windermere, and it is fitting that we end this section of the journey with two young people united on a railway station, starting on the longer journey through the rest of their lives.

GRASMERE

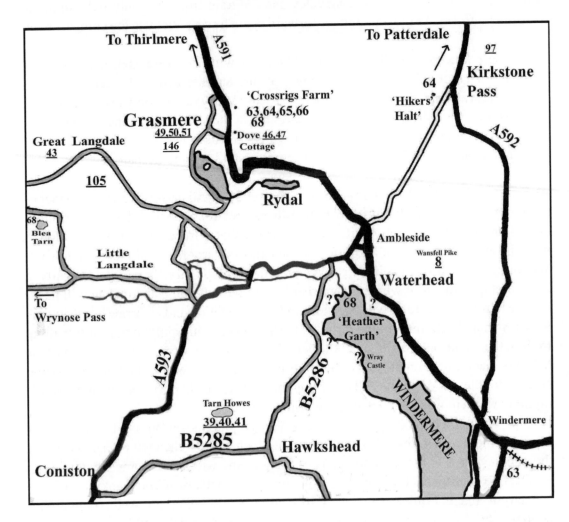

CHAPTER VI

THE ABBEY BOOKS—A GIRLS' SERIES COMES TO THE LAKES
Grasmere, Kirkstone Pass, Windermere

As we move north to the head of Windermere, to Ambleside and from there to Grasmere, it may truly be said that we are reaching the hub of the wheel from which all the major lakes seem to radiate like irregular spokes. Without doubt, Dove Cottage and the little Grasmere church of St Oswald, whose grounds contain Wordsworth's grave, are at the heart of the literary Lake District. The small town, in its magnificent setting near to the small lake with its little island and its views of Helm Crag, Silver How and Loughrigg Fell, is also a fascinating treasure house of interesting little shops.

Only three children's writers have been granted a chapter of their own in this book. They are Arthur Ransome, Geoffrey Trease and Elsie Jeanette Oxenham. Ransome's connection with the Lake District has always been universally recognised. Less widely read or studied are the works of Geoffrey Trease who, as we have seen and shall see, has much more than the Bannermere stories to identify him with Cumbria. It is time now to look at the Lake District books of 'EJO', as she is popularly called by her many devotees. The publication dates of the last four volumes correspond very closely with the years when the Bannermere novels were being written. Yet it would be difficult to find two authors more different in the worlds that they created than Trease and Oxenham. Both authors are clearly linked, nevertheless, by their love of the landscape that they describe and the effect that it has upon their central characters.

It is generally agreed that one of the most extraordinarily popular series of books for girls is the Abbey series by Elsie J Oxenham. Abbey societies are still supported in great strength in both England and Australia. The 'hard to find' Abbey books in good condition still bring enormous prices on the second-hand market (as I write this chapter a copy of EJO's *A Go-Ahead Schoolgirl* is being advertised on AbeBooks for £3,750), and even battered copies of some rarities will bring a handsome return. The abbey that features in many of the books is another one of those literary amalgams so beloved of children's authors. It is most closely based on Cleeve Abbey in Somerset, but EJO re-sited it in Oxfordshire, not far from the Buckinghamshire border. This allowed her to develop the setting and the characters which she had first introduced in the seminal story *The Girls of the Hamlet Club*.

It is almost impossible to come to a definite agreement about just how many of her eighty-seven books belong to the Abbey series. Some are entirely separate, and some belong entirely and very often contain the word Abbey in the title. Others, however, are loosely titled 'connectors', because, though the action in these stories is not centred on the Abbey, the characters in them play a part in the Abbey story in other volumes in the series. This is the case with those that have a connection with the Lake District, for **Damaris at Dorothy's (63)**, published in 1937, tells of Damaris and Rachel's schooldays in Southport long before the connection with the Abbey characters is established.

The seven books in this chapter contain the main events in the lives of the sisters Damaris and Rachel Ellerton, but the second in the series, **Maidlin to the Rescue (64)**, was written and published in 1934, three years before the first, *Damaris at Dorothy's*. This is a practice that Elsie J Oxenham repeated elsewhere, slipping backwards in fictional time to give her readers scenes from the early life of vital Abbey characters such as Jen.

Of the seven books, only four contain crucial scenes set in the Windermere, Grasmere and Ambleside district of our region under study. The others are included so that the story of Rachel and Damaris may be rounded off. Some of the books themselves are almost impossible to obtain and so I have no hesitation in narrating here in chronological order a story of the Lake District that might otherwise be lost.

The story of *Damaris at Dorothy's* begins and ends in the Lake District. In Chapter 1, the author takes the reader on board the early morning train from Windermere (that station once again) to Liverpool to share the compartment with Philippa (called Pip) as she goes away from home to a private school for the first time at the age of twelve. She is travelling alone and has been put into the care of a nice middle-aged woman called Mrs Grayson, who promises to look after her until she can be picked up by the authorities at her new school.

Pip is so excited that she can't concentrate on the book she is meant to be reading. However, she has two thoughts which cause her a lot of apprehension. The first is that she will be starting school after all the other girls, and the second is that she fears being 'bossed about' by two older girls who live near Grasmere. The girls are from a family called the Ellertons and their home is on a very small farm. Pip has never met the girls, but her worry about being controlled by two girls who happen to live in her district makes her take a snobbish attitude towards them. As she falls into conversation with her companion, she learns that the woman is in fact the mother of the head girl, Roberta Grayson. Mrs Grayson chides Pippa for her snobbishness and advises her to go to Dorothy's without any preconceptions.

It is only when the story reaches Liverpool and then transfers to the coast near Southport that we realise that, though Pip is an important character in her own right, it is really Damaris Ellerton and her sister Rachel who are at the centre of the author's concerns. In fact, in terms of the long Abbey series, Damaris becomes one of the most important young heroines, with her story occupying several of the books. The account of Damaris, Rachel and Pip's time at Dorothy's takes place outside the Lake District and mainly concerns the making and breaking of sentimental friendships in the school environment. I ought to mention at this point that EJO has an unusual but sometimes endearing tendency to give her characters additional nicknames or pet names. It can be confusing if the reader doesn't realise that Damaris is also called 'Marry' and 'Dammy' and sometimes even 'Damson'; that Rachel is also 'Ray'; and, as we have already seen, Philippa is sometimes called 'Pip', 'Pippa' or even 'Philip'. Damaris, the younger sister, is the stronger character and the school favourite. For the sake of Rachel, both Damaris and Pip get themselves into trouble and lose their school colours.

The school year ends with Rachel worrying about her matriculation examinations and about her former friend Margery, whose sister, she has just learnt, is dangerously ill. Although the once-loved Margery had completely dropped Rachel when she left school and moved on to new friendships, she now wants Rachel's moral support during her time of crisis. Having finally got over the pain of the loss of the friend to whom she had been devoted, Rachel finds herself back under the strain of the unequal friendship again. The strong emotional appeal that is contained in the letter Rachel reads in the train heading north to the Lake District is to haunt her all summer as she tries to decide how to respond to it.

The resolution to Rachel's troubles is played out amongst the mountains and lakes near Grasmere.

When Pip meets the two sisters again, it is the day on which Rachel is due to receive her matriculation results. As the summer has proceeded, Rachel has managed to write a civil and supportive letter to Margery even though the girl has killed the trust and

Grasmere and its island (photographer: Peter Lewis)

love she had once given her. A climb to Grisedale Tarn is to be Pip's initiation into the delights of exploring the mountains. Damaris, with her perceptive understanding of her sister's character, anticipates that the day will end suddenly when Rachel gets overcome by the desire to rush back to receive the fateful matriculation letter. However, before that does indeed happen, the author expands her descriptions of the surrounding scenery for the first time.

Rachel was thoughtful, lost in a dream of the future, which depended on that afternoon's post.

'The first lap! What does it do next?' Pip cried excitedly.

'You'll see!' And presently the easy green track lay behind and they were threading their way through a maze of rocks and streams, on the edge of a shelf, with a steep drop to the valley on their right.

'I can't see the path,' Pip exclaimed. 'Oh, yes, I can—over there in front. It's faint, isn't it, Ray?'

Rachel was the leader at the moment. 'It loses itself in places. But you can always see it if you look ahead. You just make a dash for the next bit. Careful here, Philip! Don't fall into the beck!'

They forded streams, and picked their way among boulders, and paused to rest and gaze up at the becks as they came tumbling down from the heights.

'We're on the side of Seat Sandal,' said Damaris. 'Fairfield is on the other side. Soon we'll see St. Sunday Crag, above Patterdale.'

… A long and very steep two miles, all through rocks and fallen stones after that first green path, brought them by a last wild scramble to a wall, which closed the valley and seemed to stand against the sky. It was built of great stones piled loosely together, and ran across from hill to hill—from Seat Sandal's flank to the slopes of Fairfield.

A big gap in the wall faced them, and Pip, panting, struggled ahead and reached it first.

'Oh, Damson! Ray! A little lake, right up on the top! Did you know?'

'That's the tarn. That's where we have lunch. Look the other way, Philip.'

Pip had been too busy with the struggle through the rocks to look round for some time. She turned, and gave a shout.

'I can see the whole world! I can see the sea!'

There seems little doubt that there is more than mere description taking place in this passage and the other shorter ones that succeed it. The path that winds upward, with its dangerous cliffs and its fading trail but also its marvellous prospects, suggests an allegory of the life of three girls. Pip is young and rash and keen to move forward, rushing onwards without too much thought. Damaris is sharply conscious of the beauty around her (she chose that particular walk!) towards which she can lead the younger girl, and

Rachel is more cautious but still determined to take on the challenges of life.

On the return journey Rachel rushes ahead to get the afternoon post and find that she has been tremendously successful. 'Rachel stood twirling her stick gaily and gazing into a future that held a care-free term, and golden Colours, and Roberta's companionship.'

But, alas, it is not to be. A very gloomy time awaits the two girls in the next book in the series, entitled ***Maidlin to the Rescue (64)***. Very soon Rachel is reflecting on their prospects after the death of her aunt:

'Now that she's gone, there's nobody but us, and not a penny to carry on the farm or help us to finish at school. And Maidlin is our cousin, and she's rolling in money, with everything she wants, and she's never even come to see us or asked how we were going to manage!'

'It sounds too bad to be true. Perhaps she doesn't understand.'

'Perhaps she doesn't—now. But why has she never written or come to see us, and the farm, in all these years? It's six years since father brought us home and Aunt Rachel took us in at Crossrigs.'

'It's eight years since Maidlin went away.'

'I know. I've been working it out; she must be twenty-two. She forgot all about her own folks, and the farm, and everything, as soon as these rich people adopted her; Lady Somebody, she lives with. I wouldn't ask her for a farthing!'

Rachel and Damaris begin their adventure.

And thus the plot of *Maidlin to the Rescue* is laid out in this short opening scene at the farm near Grasmere. Rachel's dream of the sixth form at Dorothy's was a mere illusion and Damaris can now never return to the school where she was so happy. Together they must face the world as orphans without a designated protector. From the point of view of Elsie J Oxenham's Abbey series, the connection with the south and the many characters who belong to the Abbey has been made. This is the book in which Damaris and Rachel start to join the 'family' or even the 'family firm'. Even their contrasting characters are suggested in this opening section, for Damaris is determined to think the best of people while Rachel, her senior by a year at sixteen and a half, is full of bitter reflections about Maidlin. For those who already know the story of Maidlin and have seen the title of the book, the ending is inevitable and they know that Damaris is right.

However, the pleasure of the book lies in tracing how the three main characters get to the happy ending. Practically all this book is set in the Lake District, and much of the plot is concentrated in a cottage, somewhere on a small road in the Kirkstone Pass area, that comes to be known as 'Hikers' Halt'.

Rachel and Damaris make up their minds to become young women of business and decide that the first step is to act as waitresses. They plan to take a job with Miss Baldry, whom they had known at the farm until a legacy gave her the chance to set up her own tea-rooms on the lonely pass. To avoid the clutches of their cousin Maidlin (for they are under the misapprehension that she has studiously ignored them for eight years), they run away in the middle of the night to climb the pass to Miss Baldry's. Even for ordinary working class girls the conditions would be regarded as harsh, but for two young ladies of a so-called superior class there are all sorts of humiliations that have to be faced. Elsie J Oxenham manages to create an impression of surroundings that have a rugged beauty:

> Across the road there was a field, and then the mountain wall rose steeply, strewn with fallen rocks, shutting out the world. On the other side the hill fell away to a great sweep of valley, and beyond stood range after range of hills, rising to the long ridge which hid the Pennine mountains. It was a wonderful outlook, and the cottage was wonderfully placed, at just the right spot to see it all.

However, there is a harshness and an ugliness that has to be contended with:

> It looked so very soiled and sordid, so clammy and uninviting in the grey morning mist; and surely a rest house must be inviting, if it were anything at all? Miss Baldry's little house stood with its back to the wide view and its face to the road … But this morning the valley was filled with a sea of mist and the hills lay behind a cold grey wall. The cottage seemed to cling dangerously on the edge of the precipice. 'It's hanging on by its teeth,' Damaris murmured.

To suggest that there is something 'fine' about the two girls, the author gives them legitimate excuses for grousing, but also allows an element of snobbery to creep in. Thus Damaris resents being addressed by the name 'Dammy' and Rachel is humiliated at being made to wear shorts whilst serving hikers.

Rachel had been hurt too deeply; her sense of propriety and decency, only just making itself urgently felt, was outraged to the very limit, and she loathed her costume as much as she had loved it before. Out on the high roads or up on the fells she could still have revelled in shorts, but indoors and before strangers she felt undressed and an object of derision.

Whilst Rachel's discovery of her inner self and Miss Baldry's violation of it is a legitimate ground for resentment, the author is rather ponderous in her class consciousness as she comments on Miss Baldry's rendering of Hikers' Halt as the new name for her small tea-shop.

'I'll put a bit in the local paper—"Come for tea at Hikers' Halt,"' Miss Baldry's enthusiasm was rising.
Damaris avoided Rachel's eyes, for there was quite a suspicion of ''Ikers' 'Alt' in their hostess's pronunciation.

Later, as Maidlin discusses with Jen what they can do about her cousins' future she briskly comments: 'But they're too good to be wasted serving in a shop, or typing in an office.'
It is at this point that we have to remember that these books were written for 'gels' of a certain class. The world which Rachel and Damaris are expected to occupy is one dominated by titled ladies, private schools, country dancing and, as time passes by, hordes of babies (twins especially). In spite of this, the books are about kindness rather than snobbery and about friendship and loyalty rather than privilege. Situations are still interesting and character development is still plausible, though relations with those not within the class confines of the central characters do seem to be patronising, or at best repressed as unimportant.
One of the strongest themes running through the books is a love of the English countryside.

She put down the cans for a moment's rest, and stood entranced, forgetting everything in the sight of the sun, shining on the sea of mist that still filled the great valley below the cottage. As she watched, the mist grew thin and vanished, and fields and woods appeared, with green rolling slopes, and streams like silver threads, and grey farms far away below. The hills and mountains held the mist at first; then it slipped from them also and they stood clear in the morning sunshine. The air was strong and sweet and very fresh.

By the end of the book it seems that Rachel and Damaris have come into the harbour of safety at last. Maidlin has gained a family and everyone has forgiven Aunt Ann, whose secrecy had stirred up the trouble in the first place. Everything is settled again;

Damaris has an audition
(illustration by Margaret Horder).

but Elsie J Oxenham has new shocks in store for the sisters in **Damaris Dances (65)**, published in 1940.

When the book opens, the two sisters have their futures very carefully mapped out in front of them. Rachel is to become her cousin Maidlin's secretary and Damaris is to complete her education, go to college and then become a hen- and bee-keeper on the old family farm at Crossrigs near Grasmere. But Damaris dances. Everyone who sees her is convinced that she has the talent to be a top ballerina, in spite of the fact that she is now nearly sixteen and hasn't had any formal ballet training since the age of eight.

The story tells of how Damaris feels the desire to dance blossoming within her, and how this is enhanced by the encouragement of her sister and by all who see her in action. For a while she clings to the more settled plan of becoming an 'egg and honey' lady, driving around selling her produce to the local population. However, during her stay in Annecy with Rachel, as she learns French and secretarial skills she falls under the influence of a complete balletomane, who ensures that she receives proper lessons again. One glimpse of a real ballet company in action in Aix is both daunting and inspiring. Damaris and Rachel have to reconsider their destinies. Thoughts of the Lake District are soothing and attractive:

> The bees and hens in the little fields of the Cumberland farm would be much more peaceful. Rachel suddenly saw the grey-green rocky fells, the little black-faced Herdwick sheep, the silver shimmer of Grasmere with its islet, the long slopes of Helvellyn, the cool mist and the grey veil of rain, the glory of the spring gorse and the autumn heather, of Wordsworth's daffodils by Rydal and Ullswater, the valleys with their white roads climbing up, to drop to another glittering lake, the smooth tracks among the rocks which wandered across the hill-sides, the rushing becks and the tumbling waterfalls.

She sums up her feelings:

> 'It means a lot to Marry; she loves it as I do. I've known I could only have it in holidays, if I'm working for Maid, but Marry hoped to live among

it all. I'd have gone to stay with her often. She'll have to give it up; I don't wonder she's hesitating. Home will pull her tremendously; she loves the fells so much. I expect she's thinking a lot more than she says.'

However, she recognises that for Damaris to return to this contented life without attempting to fulfil what is within her would probably leave her with a lifetime of regrets. Then Maidlin sends her cousins another piece of news, which tilts the balance towards ballet becoming Damaris's vocation:

'The Council are going to by-pass the village. It means making a big new road, and Crossrigs is right in the way.'

Rachel's response to this disturbing news is surprisingly calm and altruistic:

'Think of the narrow twisty streets in the village, and all that mass of traffic in the season! Charas, and cars, and cyclists, and crowds of hikers and climbers, all mixed up in those little roads! It's really very sensible. You couldn't expect one little farm, sitting right in the way, to be allowed to hold up a useful scheme like that. You can have your hens somewhere else. And you aren't even sure that you want them yet.'

Damaris behaves as if one of the cornerstones of her planning has been knocked away:

'I don't want them anywhere else; I'm sure of that.' Damaris frowned. 'I wanted to live at Crossrigs. I couldn't bear to settle down in a new place.'

However, the greatest impediment to Damaris trying to make her way in the world by training to become a ballerina is Maidlin. Damaris does not know how her cousin will react and she is determined never to go against the wishes of the young woman who has been so kind to them both. Before she breaks the news to Maidlin, she wants to make one last visit to the Lake District. Here the girls meet young Philippa again and pay a return visit to Hikers' Halt as paying customers. There is another interlude where Damaris is inspired to dance by music on the radio, and she feels ready at last to reveal all that has happened to her to Maidlin.

Rachel, herself released from the training to be Maidlin's secretary, knows that her real job will be to look after her sister, as Damaris embarks upon what is clearly going to be both a successful and a nomadic career.

In *Guardians of the Abbey* **(66)**, published in 1950, and *Rachel in the Abbey* **(67)**, published in 1951, the story of the sisters continues, but there is now a pause in Elsie J Oxenham's interest in the Lake District.

Damaris is indeed successful as a ballet dancer but suffers a tragic accident when

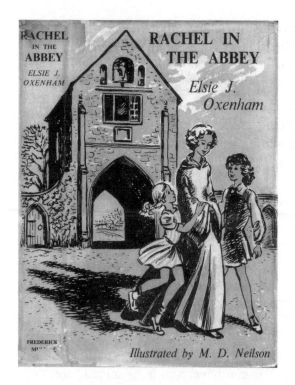

Illustrated by M. D. Neilson

bravely saving another young girl in danger on stage. It takes to page 153 of *A Dancer from the Abbey* **(68)**, published in 1953, before the story of Damaris and Rachel returns to the Lake District. This is hardly surprising, since the heart of the Abbey series belongs with the characters who live near the old Abbey itself. Rachel has become the guardian of the Abbey and the person to whom all the young girls in the Abbey world turn for advice. Damaris has taken up gardening in order to find a new interest in life. In the field near the Abbey, she has laid out two distinct gardens—called 'Wirral' and 'Windermere' after the places she loves—which she tends. The sisters are older and more ready for new opportunities and new hopes.

The main plot is based upon the conflicting passions that suddenly begin to disturb Damaris's new-found tranquillity. The first is her knowledge that she has recovered the use of her damaged leg to such an extent that she can hope to dance again. Six months of further treatment, and then practice, should allow her to return to the stage. Rachel knows that this time she will not be able to go with her as her 'sister-mother', for her duties and her inclinations are now all centred upon her life at the Abbey. The other disrupting feature in the life of Damaris is the arrival on the scene of Brian. Before long the two young people have developed very deep feelings for each other.

Both Damaris and Rachel know that in the end it will come down to a choice—the continuation of her career or marriage to Brian. Brian's new home is to be near Ambleside and his principal activity will be the development of a garden. Damaris has a choice of pathway and yet she remains undecided. The visit to her old home near Grasmere is to be the period of reflection that will allow her to come to a conclusion.

Elsie J Oxenham picks up the story as Rachel sits alone on a rocky bluff looking down on Rydal Water. Meanwhile Damaris is going for a solitary walk up to Hikers' Halt in order to tire herself out.

> Their beloved fells were as beautiful as ever, as green and brown and craggy; in places purple with heather. The lakes had their old dancing sparkle in sunshine, or were serene and peaceful at night.

Though Rachel is entirely content, she is worried about Damaris. This doesn't prevent her from realising just how much the different places in her life now mean to her. 'She knew now that much as she loved the fell country, she wanted it only at intervals, for times of refreshment such as this was meant to be …'

Rachel has even drawn inspiration for her own future stories from the landscape around her, but she would choose to write in her home in the Abbey. Her only concern is for Damaris:

> … she was restless and unhappy, unable to be still, trying always to work off the strong feeling that was surging in her. She spoke little, and was completely unlike herself.

but in terms of the pages of the book these anxieties are to be short-lived. Her sister returns with her mind made up. The decision about her future has come whilst she has been walking the hills.

> 'But suddenly I knew, and it's true. He comes first. I can't do without him. Oh, Ray, I want him.'

With her mind thus settled, Damaris wants to take a boat on Grasmere once more with her sister that night, before the morning when Brian will arrive.

> The water of Grasmere was like a sheet of dark glass as Damaris rowed gently along by the bank. Rachel in the stern was content to be quiet, now that all was well.

On the following day the sisters separate for the most momentous day in their lives. Rachel sets off to walk to Ullswater in order to spend some time at Glenridding and Patterdale before returning home in the evening. Damaris intercepts Brian in his car and they return through Ambleside and up the Langdale Valley. After lunch: '… they climbed the stony track and sat by little Blea Tarn, and Brian told her several things.'

The marriage proposal is thus made and accepted. Later that evening they meet Rachel and row out on Grasmere again and reveal that Damaris will not be married until she has made her return to the ballet. After that she will retire and become Brian's wife at Heather Garth in Ambleside. In the next chapter there is a description of the house that is to be Damaris's domain:

> The old grey house, Heather Garth, stood high on a hillside, with a wide outlook over Windermere, a shining sea. A broad terrace lay in front, and then the cliff fell away to the road, sloping gradually at each side to give a carriage-drive up to the door.

All ends happily, as you might expect, but the conclusion of the story takes us away south once again to the heartland of most of the Abbey stories. It only remains to comment that the marriage between Brian and Damaris takes place in *The Song of the Abbey* **(69)**, published in 1954, to bring the story of the two sisters to a close.

 A glance at any map of the region around Grasmere will soon tell you that many of the places mentioned in the story are accessible to those who wish to pay a visit. To hire a rowing boat and set out on to Grasmere is, as you might imagine, the easiest of options. To find the farm at Crossrigs is, of course, impossible, for all except the buildings would have been swept away by the road improvements. This road must be the A591, which leaves Ambleside, curves round the lakes of Rydal and Grasmere, and then, if you want, allows you to miss out the town altogether and proceed up Dunmail Raise to the side of Thirlmere. As you head north in this way, somewhere under your wheels, in between the two left turns of the B5287 which each take you to Grasmere with its winding lanes, must lie the fields and gardens that were to be Damaris's future. The Ordnance Survey map suggests that Hollens Farm, to the north of Dove Cottage and slightly to the east of the main road, may have inspired EJO's location of the farmhouse itself.

A walk to Grisedale Tarn is more demanding in both time and effort. One of the guide books which I consulted categorises it as 'not for beginners' and refers to 'steep climbs and an extremely steep descent'. Consult a proper guide book and local experts if you wish to make the attempt. Far better to take the journey back into Little Langdale, park near Blea Tarn and complete the walk around the little lake whilst deciding for yourself just where Brian made his proposal.

A more difficult drive is up the Kirkstone Pass, which is accessible from both Ambleside and Windermere. The fictional Hikers' Halt was most likely on the shorter and very daunting precipitous road from Ambleside, which is aptly marked on the Ordnance Map as 'The Struggle'. The only habitation is the Kirkstone Pass Inn, which stands at the junction of the main road from Troutbeck to Patterdale. From the picnic tables

Kirkstone Pass (photographer: Adrianne Fitzpatrick)

outside you can get the sort of views that Elsie J Oxenham allowed Damaris and Rachel to enjoy whilst struggling with their domestic chores.

I fear, however, that you will search in vain for Heather Garth, Brian's house somewhere on the northern shores of Windermere, for the description is so generalised that anywhere from Wray Castle on the west coast to Cragwood House on the east could have given the author her inspiration.

Grasmere, Rydal, the Kirkstone Pass and Ambleside have been key locations in this E J Oxenham survey. However, it is now time to leave these tales of the southern region so that we can return to another central location by a different route.

DERWENTWATER AND KESWICK

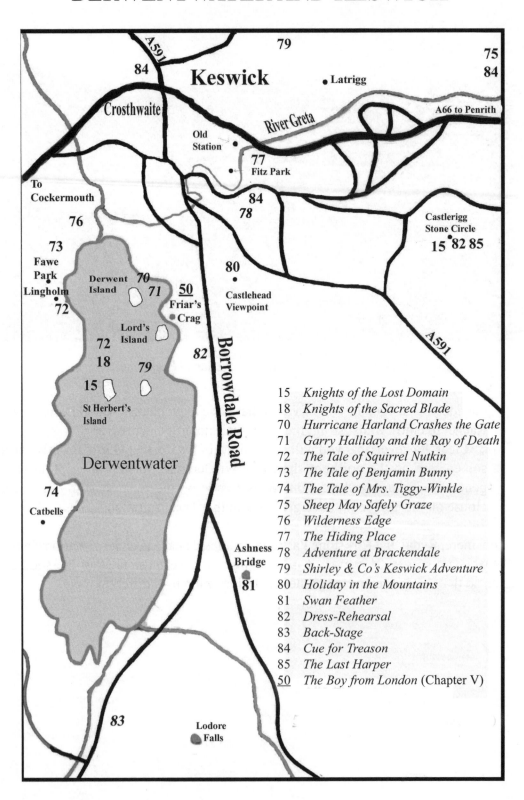

79

75
84

84

Keswick

Latrigg

Crosthwaite

River Greta

A66 to Penrith

Old
Station

77

Fitz Park

To
Cockermouth

84
78

Castlerigg
Stone Circle

76

15 82 85

73
Fawe
Park
Lingholm

80

Castlehead
Viewpoint

Derwent
Island

70

71

50

Friar's
Crag

A591

72

Lord's
Island

72

18

79

82

Borrowdale Road

15

St Herbert's
Island

Derwentwater

74
Catbells

Ashness
Bridge

81

83

Lodore
Falls

15	*Knights of the Lost Domain*
18	*Knights of the Sacred Blade*
70	*Hurricane Harland Crashes the Gate*
71	*Garry Halliday and the Ray of Death*
72	*The Tale of Squirrel Nutkin*
73	*The Tale of Benjamin Bunny*
74	*The Tale of Mrs. Tiggy-Winkle*
75	*Sheep May Safely Graze*
76	*Wilderness Edge*
77	*The Hiding Place*
78	*Adventure at Brackendale*
79	*Shirley & Co's Keswick Adventure*
80	*Holiday in the Mountains*
81	*Swan Feather*
82	*Dress-Rehearsal*
83	*Back-Stage*
84	*Cue for Treason*
85	*The Last Harper*
50	*The Boy from London* (Chapter V)

CHAPTER VII

ON THE RUN TO KESWICK

Keswick, Derwentwater, Threlkeld, Catbells, Castlerigg Stone Circle

THE town of Keswick is the northern centre of the Lake District and is backed by the mountain called Skiddaw, which dominates both Derwentwater and Bassenthwaite Lake. Although it is only three miles long, one mile wide and seventy-two feet deep, Derwentwater is often referred to as the 'Queen of the English Lakes'. Hemmed in by interesting fells on all sides, it offers a peaceful setting where you can cruise on a launch, go for a short and relatively undemanding walk and picnic in some splendid locations.

Derwentwater, the 'queen of the lakes', whose house on a wooded island has inspired several writers. In the distance are Keswick, Skiddaw and Bassenthwaite Lake
(photographer: Peter Lewis).

In this section we come first to a particular sort of book that has fallen totally out of fashion and which seems, at this stage in the development of children's literature, unlikely ever to make a return. This involves the use of a grown-up hero in children's books that form a series, where children themselves are of little consequence or even missing altogether. The stories about Biggles, Gimlet, Flame, Bill Berenger, Adam MacAdam, PC 49 and their ilk are not exactly forgotten but are certainly not widely read by the children of today. Two examples of this once popular hero type take us to the Lake District once more.

A House on an Island

'The wild and mountainous English Lake District—why it's ideal for a criminal's hide-out ...' So says Kenton, the butler, in **Hurricane Harland Crashes the Gate** (70), published in 1958, the fourth adventure of this boyhood hero recorded by the writer Tom Allum.

The two words used to describe Bill (Hurricane's real name) on the dustjacket blurbs are 'quick-thinking' and 'hard-hitting', and they do indeed seem appropriate, if rather hackneyed, terms for the man who has got used to the rough and tumble of a life spent frustrating the activities of master criminals.

The villainous Owl gloats over the securely bound Hurricane and his butler Kenton (illustration by Victor Bertoglio).

In this final book of the series, Bill and Kenton are on the trail of 'The Owl', a master criminal whose organisation Bill and Kenton have broken up in a previous book and whose attempts to re-establish himself in this one have also met with frustration. As we can see from the quotation about a criminal's hide-out, the redoubtable duo is very close to tracking this particular Napoleon of crime to his lair in the Lake District.

When the action breaks out on an island in the middle of 'Broadmere', it builds to a climax in a very exciting fashion. The Owl makes his getaway in a fast motor boat, but the author devises a face-to-face confrontation which ends with a highly satisfactory explosion.

Tom Allum's book is a well-written junior thriller whose climax just happens to take place on a lake in the Lake District. The author's greatest skill is in creating relentless and well-crafted action sequences. However, there are enough plausible details in the descriptions of lakes and islands to allow you to imagine the events taking place in the middle of Windermere or Derwentwater. All four of Tom Allum's Harland stories are worth reading for their well-controlled plots and their sheer verve and energy.

Another children's thriller with an adult hero and a Lake District background is **Garry Halliday and the Ray of Death (71)**, published in 1961.

Before the nearly unstoppable bandwagon that is *Dr Who* began to appear on BBC television screens in the early 1960s, the vital slot on a Saturday evening after *Grandstand* and before the news was filled by a children's series about a commercial airline pilot called Garry Halliday. There were five books relating to the series, and the author's name was given as Justin Blake, but this was merely a cover for the collaboration of John Griffith Bowen and Jeremy Bullmore.

The hero, Garry, was played by Terence Longden, who later also became some kind of stunt double for the Sean Connery version of James Bond in the early films. The part of Garry's friend and co-pilot was taken by Terence Alexander, who later found a niche in *Bergerac* as Charlie Hungerford, the reformed crook and father-in-law of the Jersey detective portrayed by John Nettles. The charismatic and totally hypnotic Voice, against whom Garry constantly pitted his wits, was breathed into life by Elwyn Brooke-Jones.

The view of Derwent Island from the Keswick Landings

Like the villain in the Hurricane Harland story, it has occurred to the Voice, the criminal mastermind in this story, that a remote house in the middle of an island is a good place for a secure hide-out. However, once the hide-out is detected, its very inaccessibility turns it into a trap. It seems that all the forces of law and order have to do is to throw a cordon round the island and the villain has no hope of escape. It does not prove that easy.

Garry gets on to the trail of the Voice through the intriguing idea of a piece of jigsaw. For the first three quarters of the book, Garry and his friends have been following the trail on the reverse side of the pieces of a jigsaw, as the formula for a death-ray machine is paid for on the instalment plan by some foreign revolutionaries. Having exposed the crafty scheme and arranged the round-up of the would-be insurgents, Garry turns his attention to tracking down the villain behind it all. He instructs Bill to turn the puzzle over once more so that the picture can be seen. Bill looks at it closely for the first time. Why the Voice should give away his hiding place like this defies rational analysis but it does provide the story with the opportunity for a tremendous climax.

> The picture on the puzzle was the same as the picture on the box. A lake …
> One of the islands had a house on it; you could just see the house in the puzzle. The last piece of the puzzle was one of the three pieces that made up the island. It was the piece with the house on it.

The Garry Halliday adventures are well-constructed stories which have an admirable verve in the way they are written. However, it is fair to say that the use of the Lake District setting is merely a well-contrived twist of the plot, rather than a piece of writing that conveys anything of the essence of the region.

A short walk from the centre of Keswick brings you to the boat landings at the northern end of the lake. Here you can gaze across the water to Derwent Island, where, partially concealed amongst the trees, is an eighteenth-century house. It would be the ideal place to film the events that take place in this book, and those in the 'Tarn House' mansion setting of Hurricane Harland's last adventure. Both house and island are owned and administered by the National Trust, which permits pre-arranged visits on just five days a year. Details may be found at their website.

Mention of the National Trust brings us again to the stories of the Trust's most famous benefactor—the remarkable Beatrix Potter.

Before she put down roots in Near Sawrey, a large number of her summer holidays were spent on the shores of Derwentwater. *The Tale of Squirrel Nutkin* (72), published in 1903, is really her first true Lakeland book, with the backgrounds offering views of the lake, the nearby Newlands Valley, and the slopes of the gentle fell Catbells. Most recognisably, there is a picture of St Herbert's Island, which is called Owl Island in the book, with Squirrel Nutkin paddling across to it. Many of the sketches for this tale, and the ones that followed it, emerged from six summer holidays at a house called Lingholm. However, *The Tale of Benjamin Bunny* (73), published in 1904, owes most of its scenes to a summer spent at Fawe Park, the house next door to Lingholm. A friendship with the vicar of Newlands and his daughter Lucie contributed to the creation of Lucie of Little-town in *The Tale of Mrs. Tiggy-Winkle* (74), published in 1905, in which Beatrix changed her own pet hedgehog into the washerwoman of Catbells.

 You can attempt a short walk on Catbells by travelling to the southern end of the lake either by car or by boat. A small number of parking places exist in Swinside Village and at the side of the road above Brandlehow Park. The start can also be reached by catching the Derwentwater ferry to Hawes End. There is a very clear footpath where the road is crossed by the end of the ridge. Follow the stony path up the hill; you can check you are on the right route by looking for the plaque to Thomas Arthur Leonard. Eventually you will get to a section where a broad ridge offers you an area of level land before the path rises again to the summit. After a short downhill section, a fork to the left takes you back down to the valley, where you will encounter a path by a stone wall that will guide you back down to the road.

On the Hills near Threlkeld

Let us, after this excursion into the world of grown-up adventure heroes and a brief mention of the famous animal characters of childhood, slip back to a much earlier time and a story which is based, at least partly, on the real history of England.

The story of *Sheep May Safely Graze* (75) by Phyllis Bentley, published in 1972, begins in Skipton Castle in north Yorkshire during the time of the Wars of the Roses. The hero of the book is Henry Clifford, a member of a great Lancastrian family, who falls victim to the Act of Attainder which states that all Clifford lands and lives are forfeit to the Yorkist king. As the Lancastrians lose power and Henry's father and grandfather are killed, even Skipton will not be safe from the growing acquisitions of the Yorkists. It matters little that Henry is a mere seven years of age, for all the males of the Clifford name are to be wiped from the earth.

The young nobleman is forced to flee with only a servant woman, Margery, as his protector. She is drawn to the small community of Threlkeld by the affection that she felt when young Will Angram, a shepherd, came to call over business with the sheep. Henry finds that to survive he must deny his nobility and enter an entirely different world, the world of the Lakeland shepherd. The core of the book is concerned with the way in which he adapts to his new, secret life. In the small rudimentary cottage, by the side of the River Glenderamackin, he has to learn to sleep on bracken strewn on the hard-packed earthen floor in the lean-to. Perhaps the most touching incident occurs when he finally makes friends with Tuddler, Will's shepherd dog, and discovers a companion who can help him through the lonely hours of the night.

> That somebody, even if only a dog, wanted him and welcomed him and thought well of him, was a balm to his sore heart. He put his arm round Tuddler's hairy body and drew him close, and together, snug and warm, they slept happily through the night.

Although the Lake District becomes his home, Hal is still kept informed of events in the outside world, and, rather improbably, has opportunities to observe both men who have worn the crown of England.

When the Yorkists are defeated at Bosworth, the mature Henry comes into his inheritance and meets the people of Skipton again. He promises that he will continue to be a 'good shepherd'. He may have become an illiterate labourer but he is determined to recover the education of his early youth and bind it with the lessons of life on the Lakeland fells.

Threlkeld is three miles east of Keswick, just off the A66. It is the starting point for many of the routes up Blencathra, which used to be called 'Saddleback'.

You can climb the fells and think of Hal's lonely ordeals amongst the sheep and his extraordinary meeting with the doomed Henry VI. The splendidly named River Glenderamackin still flows down the hillside, and you can look for traces of old stone cottages. Like Hal, you may even go down into Threlkeld to seek out an alehouse for a drink.

Outward Bound by Derwentwater

Like the five Garry Halliday volumes, *Wilderness Edge* **(76)**, by John Coombes and Martin Riley, published in 1992, was a spin-off from a TV series of the same name. It also continues the same theme of escape, but takes us to the early 1990s and a different form of running away to the countryside.

The basic premise is that a group of youngsters are about to spend some time at an Outward Bound centre in the Lake District. Removed from their home environment, and presented with the challenge of coping with various activities on a demanding course, it is believed that the children should begin to develop new aspects of their character. The centre at the heart of the story is based very closely on the Newlands Adventure Centre, not far from Keswick. Quite a lot of the action therefore takes place on the surface of Derwentwater and on the surrounding fells. *Wilderness Edge* suffers a little from its episodic structure but is still an interesting read.

A Family Runs Away to Keswick and Beyond

There is an incident in *The Hiding Place* **(77)** by Winifred Mantle, published in 1962,

Outward Bound canoes on Derwentwater

which suddenly transforms it from being a run-of-the-mill family story into quite a frightening thriller.

The children in the family home are being terrorised by a Mr Butt who wants to track down their elder brother, who knows too much about his criminal activities. They have taken refuge on the roof behind a gable end and watched their enemy's frustrated search through their home. No sooner have they congratulated themselves on successfully evading him than disaster strikes when the family dog comes yapping towards the intruder.

> The man gave an irritated exclamation—they could see him get angry from where they lay. Then he turned and kicked Hugo, right on the head, a kick that lifted him right into the air, and threw him to the ground again. Then, without looking at what he had done, he walked quickly away.

The dog manages to survive this incident but the reader senses that neither the author nor the villain she has created will pull any punches.

The hiding place of the title is yet another nod to one of the most famous incidents in Lake District history, the last stand of the Cumbrian Northmen against the

Normans (see Chapter IX). The story of the secret fortress has captured the imagination of Julia and Ian. While on holiday several years before, the runaway Ian found his own version of a secret hide-out, whose general whereabouts was known only to himself, his sister Mirabel and her friend, Julia. Ian only needs to remain safely hidden for a week until his uncle returns to the country to retrieve the vital evidence, and then they can go to the police. No one will be able to find him unless a member of his family betrays his secret. It is not without some horror that the reader watches the blundering progress of the children as they overcome difficulties of travel, accommodation and baby-care whilst remaining blissfully unaware that they are blazing a trail that even an idiot could follow.

There is a vivid account of the long train journey to Penrith and then the much shorter rail link to Keswick. The children are befriended by a Mrs Mackenzie, who takes a strong interest in the welfare of baby Adam. The children just accept her as a rather interfering adult, but the reader knows that her outwardly helpful manner is just a mask for something far worse. The train arrives at Keswick Station and they still can't seem to shake her off. In the end it is Norman who sits in Fitz Park as a decoy, while the others make their way to the bus station where he joins them at the last minute.

The bus that leaves Keswick Bus Station takes them on that short journey so often made by children's writers—the voyage from the real places of the Lake District, that we can all go and visit, to the fictional landscape whose features are used to expedite the story. Summermere proves to be a lake with a hidden underwater causeway and a secret inlet behind a solid wall of rock. It's what every child dreams of as a place of his or her own. Ian's stronghold is impregnable, but an attack on his family brings home the lesson that it is people who matter the most. When the crisis comes, every member of the group of children (even the savage cat) contributes to the frustration of the villains' plans.

Any stay in Keswick should include a visit to the old railway station that lies appropriately enough at the end of Station Road.

The station is still largely intact, and you can wait under the portico and stand on the edge of the platform. A society has been formed to press for the reintroduction of the service, but whilst it tackles its financial and bureaucratic mountain, you can use the path on the old track-bed as a secure route back through the town, over the river and roads, and even part of the way up the hills to such haunting locations as the Castlerigg Stone Circle. Return to Station Road and, as you walk along the pavements towards town again, you will find Fitz Park on your right. You can turn in, sit by the river and perhaps watch the cricket, and then think about how Norman gave the slip to my perfidious namesake—Mrs Mackenzie.

In the Hills above Keswick

In the 1961 book *Adventure at Brackendale* (78), Linda Peters (Arthur Catherall) may be a male author writing under a female pseudonym, but he offers to his female readers two girls with admirable spirit and determination, untainted by any male condescension. One is Avril Leresch from Paris and the other is Ann Birkett, who lives on a small farm high in the hills near Keswick. Avril has come to spend a short holiday with her penfriend, but within a day two other new arrivals in the district have transformed a quiet vacation into a heart-stopping adventure. A plane crash on the fells, with no fatalities, but with a missing passenger who has a bag of diamonds strapped to his wrist, offers the first interruption to their rural seclusion. Even more dramatically, the girls' encounter with the passenger, Bill Leaming, reveals that somewhere in the bracken of Brackendale is an escaped cougar or mountain lion. The reader's interest is sustained by the sheer pace of events and the good humour of the narrative. It is also interesting to follow yet another escape story, but with the twist that the fugitive is an animal.

Inspiration from Above—The Keswick Convention

The hills and valleys of the Lake District have proved inspirational to artists, to writers and, perhaps most powerfully of all, to those who see the hand of God reflected in the countryside around them. Now, as we move around the heart of the Lake District, we can explore just how much this scenery meant to some other writers of girls' stories. Sometimes the discovery of faith is formalised by attendance at the world-famous Keswick Convention.

The religious meeting called the Keswick Convention was founded in 1875 by the vicar of St John's church, the Reverend Thomas Harford-Battersby, and his Quaker friend, Robert Wilson. Their intention was to offer depth of insight into the Bible and into human nature and to develop 'the commitment to pass on those insights with clarity, compassion and power'. It first started as a small meeting on the vicarage back lawn and has now grown to attract over 10,000 participants during two weeks in late July and early August.

In Helen Kent's *The Mystery Prize* (8), first mentioned in Chapter I (page 12), the young heroine, Hope Harland, eventually decides to dedicate herself to God after an incident in the mist upon the slopes of Wansfell Pike near Ambleside. The power of the Convention is conveyed in this story and in at least two others written for teenage girls. Each in its way brings out the conflicting desires of wanting to run away from the commitment to God, and the mixed challenge and comfort that manifests itself when the decision is taken.

Shirley & Co's Keswick Adventure **(79)** by Dorothy Fletcher, published in 1952, was written by an author who clearly possessed deep Christian convictions. Whilst being openly didactic, it also attempts to weave an adventure into a narrative which is really about how three teenage girls come to dedicate their lives to Jesus.

In the ninety-six pages of the book there are twenty-one chapters, some of which are so brief that the reader is brought up short after just three pages. To a certain extent, this sums up the spirit of the book, for though important issues are discussed and many potentially interesting characters are introduced, nothing is gone into in any depth.

After a day spent swimming and sunbathing, the girls, Shirley, Pam and Connie, are surprised when they arrive back at their uncle's farm where they are staying and discover a newspaper headline which declares: 'Monster Seen in Derwentwater'. The three girls are demarcated from each other by their reaction to what they read. 'Pam felt that the story was true; while Connie found it difficult to make up her mind. As for Shirley, she felt the whole thing was a make-up.'

These reactions prove to be reflections of the different ways by which the girls come to accept Christianity. It is not until the end of the book that the girls discover

Jenny relaxes amongst some typical Derwentwater scenery
(from *Holiday in the Mountains*).

that the monster was probably created by the extreme heat of the day acting upon a sunken boat, which rose to the surface and then sank again. (In reality today, there are accounts by local history experts of floating islands caused by the build up of gas amongst rotting vegetation after a long period of scorching weather.)

The climax of the book comes, however, when the three girls set out to climb Skiddaw and to descend on the other side to Bassenthwaite. A fog comes down and they are soon lost. A sudden temporary lifting of the mist saves them from falling into a chasm. Shirley finds herself thinking of the words of the hymn 'Lead, kindly light' and reflecting upon how God has saved them. The ending of the book has been inevitable from the first line. By the last page Shirley, Pam and Connie are all ready to accept God into their hearts.

Holiday in the Mountains (80) by Elizabeth Mumford, published in 1947, is another book in which the Keswick Convention plays a most significant part. However, the events at the Convention are merely the starting point for the storyline, which spends a considerable amount of the book considering the consequences of what happens to Robin and Jenny, when one of them makes an unexpected public declaration of faith.

After a debilitating attack of measles, lifelong friends nineteen-year-old Jennifer and eighteen-year-old Robin manage to fit in a walking holiday in the Lake District before they go on to college in London.

When Jenny's feet become covered in blisters, both girls are glad to accept a lift from Shirley, a young widow who is staying with her sister and brother-in-law whilst she recovers from her bereavement. Together all three go to Keswick to attend the last evening of the Convention. On their way, they take in the scenery:

> The drive into Keswick was sheer joy … It was an unforgettable experience, looking down from a mountain road at the stretch of country below, the thick dark clumps of woodland dotted about green meadowland, and the wooded slopes and the rugged crags stretched above the quiet blue stillness of Derwentwater. Keswick lay in the valley—a little sheltered town under the giant flanks of the mountains. All the time, as they drove down into the town, Robin's fascinated eyes were watching the great hump of Skiddaw, chequered with varying lights and shadows, blue-green and purple.

At the meeting in the tent which follows, Robin finds that the whole equilibrium of her life has been disturbed by Jenny's sudden confession of faith.

For the first time Robin feels that she has come across something which she cannot possibly share with her friend. It is only when Shirley takes them to experience Derwentwater by moonlight that her feelings begin to moderate.

> They went to Friar's Crag, and stood at the end of the promontory, by the Ruskin Stone, looking out over the water to the bracken-covered heights of Catbells. In spite of herself Robin's feeling of 'prickliness' and anger left her, here amongst this beauty; she stood and marvelled silently at the

loveliness of the lake seen from this new viewpoint, at the stillness of the pines and the unruffled quiet of the water.

This scene provides only a brief oasis of tranquillity, for Jenny's open adoption of religion has made her feel 'hot and cross and uncomfortable'. She will not be preached at; and though the two girls enjoy the rest of their holiday, Robin finds herself continually disturbed by what has happened to Jenny. Their togetherness has been broken.

The very nature of the book ensures that she will be drawn to God just at the moment that she most needs to find him. From this point in the book the message of the story becomes more and more overt.

A return to the Lake District brings the story to its conclusion. Once again the girls attend the Convention and once again Robin feels uncomfortable with this public kind of affirmation of belief and its open, collective worship. It is only when she climbs the wooded hill of Castle Head and some lines of poetry by John Oxenham come into her mind that things begin to make sense:

> To every man there op'neth a High Way and a Low,
> And every man decideth the way his soul must go.

She reasons out all that has happened to her and begins to see her way ahead:

> Robin rose and looked across Derwentwater to the mountains. Things were not yet fully clear in her mind, but the wonder of them was dawning. Here on this green hill the thought of a 'green hill far away' came to her with a new force.

 A walk of less than two miles, which shouldn't take more than an hour, will allow you to try to relive what happened to the young heroine. From the Moot Hall in the centre of Keswick you need to walk past the cinema and St John's Church until you reach Springs Road. About two hundred yards along Springs Road, you will find a signpost pointing to a wooded hill. Enter the wood and climb the path to the summit. There you can look back down over Keswick or, with Robin's story in mind, you can experience the three green hills: the one on which you stand, the marvellous view of Catbells across the lake and the thoughts of the 'green hill' in the famous Easter hymn.

A different descent allows you to complete a circular walk by following a path to the Borrowdale Road and from there to the side of the lake. From here, it is an easy walk back past 'The Theatre by the Lake' to the town again. The other viewpoint of Friar's Crag, mentioned in several of the Lake District stories, lies on this flat return section and offers a comfortable alternative stroll along good tarmac paths.

Another Way of Finding Yourself: Ballet in the Hills

I move on now to an author whose many stories constantly tackled the theme of the importance of finding one's role in life. As these books also usually involved finding one's partner in life, they could perhaps be categorised as young adult romances.

Three books by Lorna Hill in her famous Sadler's Wells series, *Swan Feather* **(81)**, *Dress-Rehearsal* **(82)** and *Back-Stage* **(83)**, all have sections of their stories set in the Lake District, near to Keswick.

In the first of these, the reader is shown Sylvia Swan, recently promoted to the giddy heights of ballerina, ultimately achieving happiness in her personal life as well. The final act in her journey to maturity is played out on a little pack-horse bridge above Derwentwater. 'They had been to Watendlath, that enchanting hidden valley above the lake, and now were on their way down to their hotel on the shore.'

A discarded feather which flutters over the parapet of the bridge into the stream below marks the end of an unhappy passage in her life, and she can walk into the future with her new husband. You will note that I have suppressed the details of both the significance of the feather and the identity of the bridegroom. The Lake District content of *Swan Feather* **(81)**, published in 1958, can be found in no more than two pages. It would be grossly unfair to spoil the bulk of the story, set in Newcastle and

The feather is cast from this famous bridge into the water below.

Northumberland, when the book is readily available in a recent reprint and on the second-hand market.

 Another splendid walk can take you to the site of this crucial moment in Sylvia's life. Catch the launch to the Ashness landing stage, and then, taking care as you cross the main Borrowdale Road, you can enter the steep road to Watendlath. After a short uphill climb, you can stand on perhaps the most photographed and painted pack-horse bridge in the Lake District. This is surely the one that Lorna Hill was describing on the last pages of her novel. It's worth going that little bit further up the steep road until you get to Surprise View, where the whole prospect of Derwentwater, the long arm of Skiddaw and, on a clear day, the distant Bassenthwaite is laid out before you.

Dress-Rehearsal **(82)**, published in 1959, offers a much more substantial slice of Lake District life and has as its focus the young Nona Browning, a foundling child with severe disabilities who finally fights her way through to happiness and a useful life in the world of ballet. Over half the book is spent in Newcastle, but the events that are to rescue her from her life as a back-street waif will all take place near Derwentwater and Keswick.

As a final holiday before she starts work as a maid to an uncaring and unpleasant master and mistress, Nona has been sent to an Orphaned Children's Holiday Camp on the eastern shores of Derwentwater. When the special bus pulls into Keswick, Nona drinks in the scene:

Vicky and Nona meet in the famous stone circle (illustration by Esmé Verity).

> The bus inched its way through the crowds of tourists milling around Keswick's narrow streets, and in the market-square, for it was Saturday, and Market Day. The stalls with their fruit and flowers made a bright splash of colour against the grey stone houses and shops. The quaint Moot Hall in the middle of the square gave the little lakeland town a German look.

During the week that follows their arrival, the children join in all the normal activities pursued by holiday visitors; but for Nona the pinnacle of her happiness is witnessing the performance of a special ballet called *Planetarium* in the Castlerigg Stone Circle.

Lorna Hill crams in all the details you could wish, to conjure up a magical scene of dancers representing the sun, moon, earth and all the planets performing a ballet at midnight amidst what she calls the Druids' Stones, whilst the mountains of Skiddaw and Blencathra look on from the shadows. One of the performers is Vicki Scott, the only daughter of Veronica Weston, the heroine of the Wells series.

 A visit to the Castlerigg Circle is definitely worthwhile, for, as you will see, several other books also have essential scenes laid there. For those less active, there is limited roadside parking near the site, but a walk from Keswick town centre will only take you a couple of hours. There are thirty-eight stones of which thirty-three are still standing. A further ten form a rectangular enclosure inside the ring. Surrounding the stone circle is the greater circle of the hills that gives the place its otherworldly feel.

It is inevitable that the privileged Vicki and the downtrodden Nona should meet.

In a strange way these two contrasting characters are linked by an almost desperate desire for freedom. All that Vicki yearns for is to escape from a career in ballet, whereas what Nona wants most is to find her way into the activity that for a long time has meant everything to her. At the same time, Vicki is fighting off the attraction that she feels for Jon Craymore, in whose parents' house she is staying during her performance near Derwentwater.

Nona's holiday ends with her being dropped off at Rake House, the grim and forbidding mansion on the Borrowdale Road out of Keswick. It is here she is to become the domestic servant for which the training in the orphanage has prepared her. The Hunters prove to be selfish and unimaginative rather than actively cruel, but Nona's spirit is broken on the first night when she is left alone in the gloomy and neglected mansion. As a thunderstorm cascades down the mountains she runs out into the darkness in a panic. Fortunately, she also runs into Vicki, and her life suddenly begins to take a turn for the better. The rest of the book details the extraordinary journey that the two girls make back to Newcastle in time to be ready for the dress-rehearsal of the title.

Lorna Hill had made Keswick her home after her clergyman husband's retirement from his parish in Matfen, Northumberland, and there are many glimpses of local scenes too detailed to include in this brief description. Knowledge of the surrounding mountains allows her to return to the same scenes for a brief but significant interlude in the next book, *Back-Stage* (83), published in 1960. This time she creates a winter scene that has little to do with the main theme of the book, her perennial one about how young people have to find their way to satisfaction in both earning a living and choosing a life partner.

In this story, Jon Craymore and Vicki Scott, now in their late teenage years, take Anna, the nominal heroine of the story, north to their home county of Northumberland. They travel via the Lake District as winter closes in on it. You can read about the scenes near Windermere in Chapter V on page 71.

They spend the night in Jon's family home near Keswick, and Vicki tells Anna about each of the local mountains in turn. Though they have come there on many occasions, Jon and Vicki are filled with enthusiasm for the place and declare that every time they come they get a fresh view. This time they are determined to climb Great Gable.

Jon's preparations for climbing the peak are formidable. Anna is slightly sceptical of the need for all his equipment and his stores. The incidents in the chapter that follows, 'Climbing Great Gable', are enough to change her mind. The lack of preparation of two female hikers who set off in high heels and Wellington boots is bound to lead to trouble. There follows a detailed description of how Jon, Vicki and Anna first climb Green Gable and then set off for the higher peak. Then the weather closes in and they manage to rescue Gladys, the first of the two silly girls. Jon takes charge completely and the girls are sent off to phone for the Keswick Mountain rescue team.

> 'Oh, and you'd better rope together, the three of you, as a precaution.
> The rocks are iced, and it's like a skating rink! We don't want any more
> broken legs.'

In her detailed and laudatory account of the activities of the volunteers of the rescue service, Lorna Hill's narrative reminds one of the efforts of the hikers in Winifred Finlay's *Peril in Lakeland* **(104)** (see page 140). Indeed, the two writers have more than this in common, both being from the north east and both having started their careers by producing stories for their daughters during the shortages of the Second World War. The difference between the two is that Finlay's British stories slot more comfortably into the juvenile area of the readership, involving no more than platonic friendships and uncomplicated relationships with members of the opposite sex. For Lorna Hill, however, romance was the key to much of her success, and the prospect of the long-term outcome of feelings and impressions developed during youth was meant to sustain the involvement of readers over several books. Yes, series literature is different. *Back-Stage* may be the story of Anna but it is also a vital part of the longer and more complicated saga about the relationship between Vicki and Jon.

In common with most other Lake District writers, Lorna Hill uses moments of danger to show the intuitive understanding and trust that often lie hidden beneath the superficial conversations and trivial misunderstandings that can get in the way of true happiness.

Such thoughts lead us inevitably to some of the more dramatic tales set around Keswick. However, unlike the two thriller stories that opened this section, two skilful authors of the next books were determined that the reader should be able to follow every step of the way. Geoffrey Trease and Julian Atterton may distance their stories from the modern day reader by hundreds of years of history, but they are meticulous in using real pieces of the landscape to convince us of the plausibility of their tales.

Traitors in the Hills

Cue for Treason (84) by Geoffrey Trease, published in 1940, is a story of Elizabethan England that used to be a relatively common text in the secondary years in English classrooms. It was even a set book for young people in Canada. It is still quite easily available on the second-hand market, and thus this account will suppress many of the details. I can say without hesitation that there is nothing better than reading it yourself.

It is the story of Peter Brownrigg, an ordinary boy from the slopes of Blencathra near Keswick, and what happens one night when he joins his father and their neighbours in an act of rebellion against a local greedy landowner.

After a night of high drama, it becomes the story of two runaways, Peter and Kit, one of whom is definitely not quite what we first expect. The story moves quickly from Peter's school in Keswick to an inn in the market place of Penrith and an appearance on stage in Kendal. Then from the wilds of Cumberland we are taken the length of England in the company of strolling actors and see the precarious and sometimes downright unpleasant life that they led. The scenes in Elizabethan London are particularly engrossing, and a certain William Shakespeare enters the plot. Chapter 14

The valley between Skiddaw to the left and Blencathra to the right is the most probable location for Lonsdale in *Cue for Treason*.

opens with the words: 'That was how I entered the Secret Service of the Queen.'

The return to Cumbria brings a new set of dangers for Peter and Kit, and new delights for the reader. We get to know the mountains, the lakes and islands. In particular we witness the events in and around a lonely peel tower on the fellside between Keswick and Penrith. There are small islets to be found on the surface of Ullswater, and Geoffrey Trease gives you a very clear idea of what it is like to be imprisoned on one (Norfolk Island is the one that fits the account best—see the Ullswater Map in Chapter VII) and then attempt to swim ashore when you are still groggy from a blow on the head. The famous edges on Helvellyn are daunting at the best of times, and to be pursued up and across them by men who can't afford to let you live turns them into places of sheer horror.

Even the friendly town of Keswick holds threats that lie in wait for the unwary. The death of a friend, kidnap and escape, and a race to London to save the life of the Virgin Queen follow pell-mell to an unusual but highly satisfying climax. You too can travel in imagination on horseback down the length of Thirlmere, past Grasmere and Rydal Water and alongside the interminable waters of Windermere, counting yourself lucky that you won't be glancing over your shoulder for the men who are determined to catch and kill you. It really is the best of chases.

The story is made all the more appealing because the young central characters are depicted warts and all. Peter, the narrator figure, reveals his own weaknesses and shortcomings. Kit, his companion, suffers from both pride and vanity. The picture given of Queen Elizabeth is also not idealised, and some of the villains can be respected for the cause they support in total conviction.

The energy of the book is undeniable. If you have never read it and you have grown to adult years, it is still possible to enjoy the uncluttered plot, the marvellous pace and the brilliantly sketched scenes of countryside adventure and London squalor.

The Songs of the Last Harper

However, it is fitting that we end this section of the journey with a series of references to the junior historical novels of Julian Atterton. In *The Last Harper* (85), published in 1983, the final chapters about the kingdom of Rheged take us to Keswick and to the stone circle where the midsummer fires of fertility will be lit. The narrator, Gwion, gazes up at Blencathra and thinks of the way in which even the names of the mountains will change and 'Urien and Rheged will mean nothing unless …'

The continuation dots at the end of the word 'unless' then lead on to the thought that he is the harper who will compose the song which will keep the names alive, and the deeds of his companions in men's thoughts, so long as songs are sung and tales are told in the future.

> Already the whisper of a tune and a cluster of words were making a pattern in my head. I would sing of the taking of Dun Guayrdi, I would sing of the riding of Urien.

Julian Atterton, of course, fulfils his own prophecy by writing this book which tries to tell us of the people who once lived, loved and died in the Lake District. He has become the harper himself.

His two books about the quests of Simon de Falaise show an even deeper love and understanding of many Lake District landscapes. In both **Knights of the Sacred Blade (18)** and **Knights of the Lost Domain (15)** he presents the reader with many different views of the countryside around Derwentwater.

The celebrated St Herbert's Isle is first visited by Simon in *Knights of the Sacred Blade*. He is searching, with his friend Aimeric, for the solution to the riddle that he first uncovered at Lindisfarne, the island off the north Northumberland Coast. The mystery can only be unravelled by a visit to the holy hermit who lives out his lonely days on the islet in the middle of Derwentwater. For Simon, his first sight of the lake comes as a surprise. He describes it as 'a lake as blue as the sapphire on Thurstan's ring'. Thurstan is the Archbishop who has sent the two men on their urgent and dangerous mission. In the event Simon and Aimeric the scholar glean part of the information they need and then spend an uneasy night on St Herbert's Isle before they are rushed quickly back to the shore so they cannot be trapped by a gathering storm. The conclusion to their story lies back in the north of Northumberland.

In the west coast section of the sequel, *Knights of the Lost Domain* (see pages 19–21), we followed the first part of the journey of Simon, Orm and Aimeric in the blighted lands between Carlisle and Millom. This second story, set once again during King Stephen's troubled reign, records how Simon and his companions attempt to track down the secret of the Runes of Alnerdal. As they are pursued by the ruthless Fitzduncan, their odyssey takes them once more to Borrowdale, to Derwentwater and finally to the stone circle. First, however, it is by the side of Derwentwater, before they slip once again across to the hermit's isle, that Simon asks Adele, the girl he has come to love, the most important question of their lives. Later it is at the centre of the stone circle that the villainous Fitzduncan finally begins to embrace his extraordinary destiny.

The harper's thoughts in *The Last Harper* have come true. The old names have gone. What was once Cadair Owain has now become Skiddaw. The Celtic kingdom of Rheged has disappeared. The world has changed.

However, a perceptive reader of the two Knights stories can still detect the universal messages of love, hatred and reconciliation in the lives of Simon, Adele and Fitzduncan and in what Julian Atterton declares that the runes were saying. The mysterious stone circle remains. And we can conclude that a skilful and sensitive writer can still bring to life the world of these distant people and the places that meant so much to them.

ULLSWATER AND PENRITH

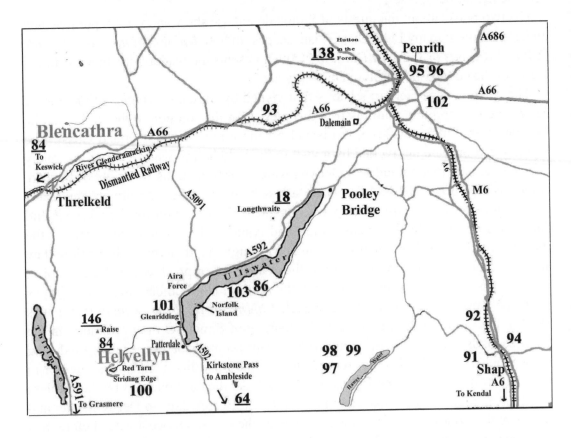

86 *The Runswick Treasure*
91 *Strangers at Snowfell*
92 *Smoke Over Shap*
93 *Railway Yarns*
94 *Pony Thieves*
95 *Her Kingdom*
96 *The Lakeland Mystery*
97 *Hunter of Harter Fell*
98 *Lakeland Gray*
99 *Vix*
100 *Razor Eyes*
101 *Amanda at the Manor*
102 *The Rebel*
103 *Silver Guard*

18 *Knights of the Sacred Blade* (Chapters II and VIII)
64 *Maidlin to the Rescue* (Chapter V)
84 *Cue for Treason* (Chapters VII and VIII)
138 *Quest for Romance* (Chapter X)
146 *The Clue in the Castle* (Postscript)

CHAPTER VIII

ANOTHER WAY TO THE LAKES

Ullswater, Helvellyn, Kirkby Stephen, Mallerstang, Penrith, Shap

Is Ullswater the perfect lake? It is about eight miles in length, and bends and twists its way from Pooley Bridge to Glenridding. It has a mixed shoreline of gentle green fields and intriguing woods but also sheer rock faces rising from the water. Around it are the spectacular mountains, which on sunny days stand out with crystal clarity and on misty days hide themselves threateningly in ominous clouds. It is the lake of sudden changes, with the long reaches of calm water which one minute mirror the fells and the sky, and the next are first ruffled and then churned into whitecaps by the rush of wind from the Kirkstone Pass.

Riding into the Setting Sun—by the Banks of Ullswater

The plot of ***The Runswick Treasure*** (86) by George Norman, published in 1949, reverses the normal flow of events that one finds in a typical children's adventure story. For once the trail, which starts in the Lake District, leads away into another direction, in fact to another country.

The opening of the book is a delightful account of what it is like to ride across the old A66 into the rays of the setting sun. Two young apprentices, Don and Mike, have piled their motorcycles with camping gear and collapsible canoes and set off after work rather than lose a day of their projected holiday by the side of Ullswater.

Their campsite is a secluded one. When he wakes in the morning, Mike can look across the lake towards Ulpha's Tower on the hillside above the waterfall of Aira Force. The first morning is full of comfortable holiday routine as they paddle down the lake to Patterdale in order to purchase their provisions. On their way they stop at one of the small islands, perhaps the one used as a temporary prison for Peter Brownrigg in ***Cue for Treason*** (84). Later they land near St Patrick's Well outside Glenridding, and Mike watches the cars on the way to the Kirkstone Pass whilst Don goes shopping. Their return journey is uneventful,

Highway robbery

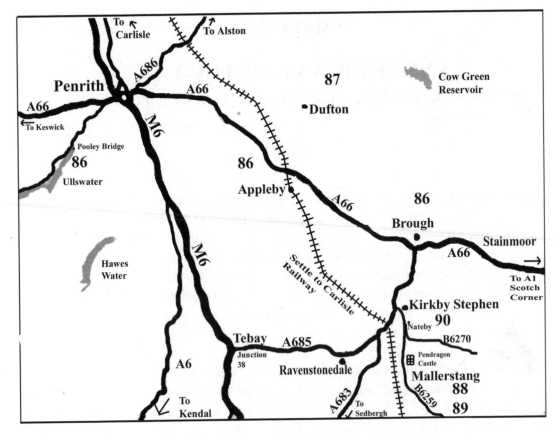

86 *The Runswick Treasure*
87 *The Secret of Hollow Hill*
88 *The Farm in Mallerstang*
89 *River Trail*
90 *The Hollow Land*

Brough, Kirkby Stephen, Mallerstang and Penrith

though there are clear signs that the wind is getting up and that a storm may be imminent.

And so it proves. There is a very convincing description of what it is like to try and sleep in a small tent as the weather begins to rage around outside. When they look out in the early morning, they are appalled to see a yacht adrift on the rough water of the lake. They know that it is their job to try and save it from crashing into the dangerous rocks. Their flimsy canoes and the power of the wind make this venture very hazardous. However, they are relieved that they made the attempt when they discover an injured man lying unconscious in a heap on the cockpit floor. If the yacht had gone down, then the man would have surely died.

The rescue completed, the boys wait several days for the injured man to recover and to tell them exactly what had happened. When he does, Don and Mike are invited to join an expedition to reclaim the Runswick fortune by a trip to Norway which will occupy the bulk of the rest of the book. There is one further scene of highway robbery by the side of Ullswater before the story moves abroad and builds towards its climax in a lonely cave.

Aira Force is one of the most popular destinations in the Lake District and a huge car park has been provided by the National Trust for those who wish to visit it. Naturally, the most spectacular time is after a particularly heavy period of rain. Unfortunately, this makes the well-marked path leading up to it very slippery. There are stone footbridges both above and below the falls, but care is needed at all times. The 'Ulpha's Tower' referred to in the book can only be Lyulph's Tower (mentioned in one of Sir Walter Scott's longer poems), which is a castellated gothic folly of a house once designed to be a shooting box. As for Patterdale and St Patrick's Well, it is said that St Patrick baptised several of the inhabitants of the dale now styled Patterdale at the well to which his name has been attached. This well is now to be found by the roadside a mile and half north of the village centre.

Underground Adventure between Brough and Penrith

In *The Secret of Hollow Hill* (87) by Garry Hogg, published in 1950, the story is set to the north and east of the main Brough to Penrith road. Nowadays, this is the notorious trans-Pennine A66, but Hogg's children clearly lived in a much quieter world where they could cycle for miles and only be overtaken by an elegant Frazer Nash sports car.

Much of the action takes place on and under the hills near the very real Dufton Pike and Murton Pike, and the 'hollowness' of the hill of the title is a testimony to the large-scale mineral mining that used to go on in this area of the countryside many centuries ago. The three children, Jonty, Nat and Penelope, have all the most important ingredients for the holiday adventure well in place by the end of the first chapter. They enjoy gargantuan meals, exercise their capacity for poking their noses into strangers' business, and discover a deserted mine which seems worth investigation.

The book falls naturally into two themes. Strangely enough, the frustrating of deadly rivals is treated as the less important of the two plotlines. The races down the hillside and along country roads, the imprisonment and escape from the enemy's headquarters and the climax in the underground tunnels (roof-falls included) are all part of the standard equipment for this sort of plot. Garry Hogg deals with these aspects in a highly competent but unremarkable fashion. He throws himself wholeheartedly, however, into the description of all the different ways in which the three children set about preparing some bayrites samples, to help an eccentric mineralogist. He is meticulous in the way he describes the building of the channels and sluices so that the children can harness the power of the mountain beck. The book remains an uneasy mixture of the down-to-earth and the downright improbable, but you can see that the author had some instinct for the child reader's relish for a basis of practical reality in a world that is largely imaginary.

The Special Farm

If we abandon for a while the track of the A66, the 'most dangerous road in the north of England', and turn south on to the A685 at Brough, we will find ourselves on the road to Kirkby Stephen and the countryside that features in *The Farm in Mallerstang* (88) by Marjorie Lloyd, published in 1956.

This rarely found and beautifully written book is probably the most clearly located of all the stories referred to in these pages. It records and celebrates the events of one year on a small farm in the Vale of Mallerstang, situated at the head of the River Eden near to the little market town of Kirkby Stephen. The dedication at the front indicates very strongly that it was deliberately based on a real farm and that the author's fictional characters were drawn from very close observation of real people. There are no outsiders. There is no adventure beyond the events of everyday existence and the passing of the seasons. To us, nowadays, unless we live in such a small community, it is a glimpse of a way of life that has perhaps gone for ever. Yet *The Farm in Mallerstang* does not have the cold and musty flavour of a social document about life fifty years ago; it is very much the story of one girl, young Anne Tyson, and the way in which she shares her life with the readers from the beginning of the New Year to the Christmas at the end of it. In a way, it is also about happiness.

The weather plays a large part in this narrative. If the young reader wants to know what it is like to spend a series of days snowed up and cut off from the world, then this is the book that tells you. The sensation of dipping your feet into the waters of a cool tarn after days of sweltering heat is also recreated for your refreshment, as is the excitement of the torrential downpour that sends the upper reaches of the River Eden into a frightening spate. If you want to feel part of an old-fashioned and yet realistic Christmas, then you would enjoy reading about the family's ritual climb for holly, the mammoth baking of mince pies and the Young Farmers' Choir that visits every house in the community on Christmas Eve and finishes by disposing of the aforementioned pre-baked feast! These events are all seen through Anne's eyes, though the narrative is exclusively in the third person. She is secure in the heart of her family, safe in her rugged but friendly community, and towards the end of the book Anne's reflections occasionally reach out to include the reader in a world without sophistication or artifice.

Mr Burra was called on, as always, for a solo, and sang in the soaring, silvery tenor voice that went so surprisingly with his weather-beaten face and his bluff figure.

As he sang, Anne, from her perch on the window seat, let her eyes wander happily round the room, gathering in all the details to remember (as she told herself) for ever ...

The unlikely marriage between the hired hand Jem Longmire and Martha Lambrigg, the woman who helps Mrs Tyson with the household chores, provides a focal point for the long summer on the farm. Anne's role as bridesmaid presents the reader with the attractiveness of simplicity and the supremacy of practicality over sentiment. No new dress is bought, and her head-dress is home made by Anne's mother, but appropriate.

She had twined forget-me-not and cornflowers and blue scabious (just the colour of the dress) on to a fine, wire ring, and it fitted Anne's head like a thin, fragile crown.

Though the practicalities of maintaining the farm are always in the background of the story, it is really the world of the children that is at the centre. The reader can recognise the descriptions of the local landmarks such as Mallerstang Edge and Wild Boar, the hump-backed bridge over the Eden and the road to Ravenstonedale, but more engrossing is the account of their daily journeys to school.

This particular year is a special one for the Tyson family, for it looks very likely that their father will actually buy them the hill pony that they have always craved. As the special sales day of the horse fair draws near, the children become imbued with excitement. The men begin to develop their 'wooden' expressions so essential for a successful bid at auction. Anne becomes so excited and nervous at the sales ring that she has to leave to go to her quiet spot by the river.

The pony that is finally chosen reflects all the attributes of the story itself. The underlying kindness and practicality of the Tysons' attitude to their livestock is enshrined in the advice that Mr Tyson gives his children as they wait impatiently for the young horse to be walked back to their farm:

'Now take it quietly when you see them,' was their father's advice. 'Don't overwhelm her to begin. You'll make friends all the sooner if you go about it gently.'

The children agree amongst themselves that the new acquisition will be called 'Lady Anne'. It reflects a part of their heritage that we might have thought they took for granted. The tourist might be led to this remote part of the Lake District by a desire to visit the ruins of Pendragon Castle, which lie at the bottom of their lane, and to which they pay scarcely any attention. However, the traditions run deep:

Years ago Lady Anne Clifford came riding through these parts, building and rebuilding a chain of castles along the edge of the fells—Brougham and Croglin and Lammerside and their own Pendragon near the bottom of the lane. She was a very great lady in those times; and they still, to this day, think well of her in Mallerstang.

The name is her brothers' choice, and they see no contradiction in their new pony being given the same name as their sister. After all, 'Anne' and 'Lady Anne' are quite different. However, in this book Marjorie Lloyd makes it the crowning moment of Anne's happiness, and a fitting point for us to leave this ordinary and remarkable story.

 Just the ruined base of a great tower is left at Pendragon Castle, which according to legend is the place where Uther Pendragon, King Arthur's father, died. The castle was built next to the River Eden in the Vale of Mallerstang in the late twelfth century, probably by Hugh de Morville, one of the knights who killed Thomas Becket in Canterbury Cathedral. The remains of Pendragon Castle are on private land but may be accessed by a gate on the B6259, which runs down the Mallerstang Valley.

In *River Trail* **(89)**, also by Marjorie Lloyd, published in 1970, we find that just around the corner from the Tysons, it seems, are an equally charming family called the Harrisons. Keld, the water bailiff's cottage where they live, stands on a knoll above the River Eden in Westmorland; and for young Libby Harrison and her brothers, the path along the river bank is the way to the village and beyond. Once again, Marjorie Lloyd writes a story about a small village, its people and its animals, both domesticated and wild; the minor tragedies and triumphs that loom and fade as the long hot summer evolves into the new autumn term. The last page of the story records Libby's thoughts about all the ways in which her world might change if she agrees to accept the bicycle suggested by her father:

And suppose that some lovely morning in June, otters were playing in the river below the hole in the bank—and she, jogging and bouncing down the dusty field path, knew nothing about them!

The decision is soon made.

'No bicycle,' Libby said, quite certain now. 'I'd rather keep to the river bank.'

More Incomers and Locals near Kirkby Stephen

The nine short stories in *The Hollow Land* **(90)** by Jane Gardam, published in 1981, are bound into a cohesive narrative by being set in the same precise area of the countryside and by involving the characters from the same two families, particularly two boys, Bell Teesdale and Harry Bateman. The nearest town of any size is Kirkby Stephen, and the pass of Stainmore, to be found on the A66, one of the most significant local features. However, the stories centre on the farms and cottages in the tiny communities such as Mallerstang and Nateby.

It is a book full of interesting episodes, the more conventional ones including the day when Bell and Harry get trapped in the old mine workings. Perhaps the most magical is when Bell, in the depths of a northern winter, takes Harry for what he calls an 'icicle ride'. The beauty of Jane Gardam's description of what the freak weather conditions have produced is enhanced by Bell's feeling that he is somehow connecting with the world of his grandfather, who several years before had shown him the same rare and extraordinary sight.

It is with the people, however, that Jane Gardam is certainly most concerned. With a book that is still readily available it would be unfair to deny you your chance to meet them yourself in their proper context, and so no more will be said, other than to promise that each of the stories brings a different reward.

The area may be on the very fringes of Cumbria, but *The Hollow Land*, *The Farm in Mallerstang* and *River Trail* demonstrate that it, too, has its very own special qualities which these three unconventional children's stories bring out so well.

Railways and Stations

But now let us get to Penrith and beyond by plunging into a very different story called **Strangers at Snowfell (91)** by Malcolm Saville, published in 1949.

The express from Euston is rushing north through the night on its way to Scotland. It is the middle of winter, the dark days between Christmas and the New Year, and a blizzard has suddenly swept down over the Lakeland fells. A steam train caught in the snow on Shap summit, a group of children in a compartment, a young man on the run, an unpleasant pursuer in a camel-coloured coat, and, in a lonely cottage near the track, a young girl whose life is made miserable by the cruelty of her aunt—these are the ingredients that go into the make-up of Malcolm Saville's adventure, in the Jillies series of stories.

Mandy, Prue and Tim Jillions, together with their friends Guy and Mark Standing, are the kind of fictional children who are always stumbling into the middle of adventures. Unlike Enid Blyton's Famous Five series, however, these books have strong delineation of character and excellent descriptions of landscape. The wider age-range of the children, from Tim at eleven to Guy at seventeen, offers a richer tapestry of character and personalities for the reader to enjoy. In particular, as the series develops, the author is careful to promote the mutual attraction that begins to develop between the slim, pretty and vivacious Mandy, who is sixteen, and the shy but strong Guy. Part of the appeal of the books is the contrast between the almost habitual bickering and bantering of Mandy and Guy, and those rarer moments where they betray the affection and respect they feel for each other.

The plot is the common one in children's adventure literature of the scientist who has discovered a formidable secret that must on no account be seized by a foreign power. In this case, Dr Thornton has chosen to carry out his researches in the small farm cottage at Snowfell near the village of Shap. Having made his tremendous breakthrough, Thornton suddenly becomes aware that he is being watched, and summons his son, Nicholas, from London to help to reassure him. It is on the night train north that Nicholas, suspecting he is being followed, makes the acquaintance of the Jillies and asks for their help in his attempts to evade the man in the camel coat.

Saville builds up the tension in the corridor and small compartments very effectively and then suddenly complicates the situation by having the train become snowbound some two miles from Shap Station. Guy wakes up to a changed world.

> Directly below them the snow was piled against the side of the train. Guy saw at once that they were on an embankment, but how high they were above the surrounding country it was impossible to say. No tree, no building, and no living thing was in sight—only a white waste of snow stretching up and up towards a horizon bounded by the rolling outline of desolate hills.

Little does he realise that soon he and Mandy are going to have to set out into this desolate world and that the blizzard is to return. The Jillies have to cope with the villains and the conditions on their own until the weather breaks.

The Jillies books are still not too difficult to obtain and so the final unravelling of the plot will be left to be discovered.

More than 120 years before the story played out in Malcolm Saville's *Strangers at Snowfell*, some real dramatic events were being enacted on the lonely fells near Shap summit. These were the incidents connected with the building of the Lancaster to Carlisle section of the railway itself. In **Smoke over Shap (92)**, published in 1975, Margaret Potter has blended together a mixture of both fact and fiction as she describes how Locke, the designer, and Brassey, the contractor, combined their efforts to push through their railway scheme for the west coast main line against all the odds. Not all the difficulties to be faced are with the terrain to be covered, for the people of Westmorland and Cumberland are divided about the coming of the railways, and Ralph Rawlings, a large landowner and a powerful man in the community, is determined to stop the iron rails by whatever method has to be used.

The story is crammed with incident, including explosions, floods, the collapse of viaducts, and terrific landslides. However, the author has stayed within the framework of those things that are known to have happened; she has merely devised her own human element to provide a coherent narrative.

More vaguely located, although encompassing details of the early railways in the north of England, are the connected short stories in **Railway Yarns (93)** by Thompson Cross, published in 1936. In particular the story called 'Changing the Luck' brings out many of the hazards faced by those who built and maintained the lines in the northern hills.

Another book to which we must give only a brief mention, for it has recently been published, is **Pony Thieves (94)** by Julia Cotter. This is a story first written in the 1940s, after the Second World War, and finally published in 2003. The opening pages describe the warmth of an arrival on what can only be Penrith Station, as Clarissa and Caroline come home for the holidays and are greeted by their younger brother and their father on the platform. At home their mother awaits them, with all the dogs and horses that make up their idyllic world in the Eden Valley. From the title of the book you can deduce what is going to shatter their feelings of happiness and security.

There is also a key scene of farewell on Penrith Station in **Her Kingdom (95)** by Amy Le Feuvre, published in 1929.

More bad luck in *Railway Yarns*

It is not often that a work of juvenile fiction actually begins with the heroine getting married. Nevertheless, it falls within the scope of this guide, because the publishers included it in their Fortune series which styles itself 'popular children's adventure and school stories'.

Underlying the hardly surprising plot of a stepmother coming to terms with rebellious children is a strong, and at times overwhelming, concern with the effect of religion upon one's life. This time there is no reference to the formal influence of the Keswick Convention, but the direct effect of landscape upon feelings is attributed once again to God's plan for each of us in this world.

Anstice Barrett has led a comfortable life in a small country village in Norfolk. Her father's death has plunged her life into financial crisis, for he has so mismanaged his affairs that there is no money left to live on. At her older second cousin's persuasion, she prepares to enter into a loveless marriage with Justin Holme, a rich widower. He needs someone to take charge of his three children who have driven out a succession of teachers and governesses. He puts the proposition bluntly in front of her:

> 'You will not be stinted in money and you will have a free hand in most things … I won't suggest a Church Service, as it is strictly a business arrangement between us and nothing more.'

The main scenes of the story are set in Butterdale Manor, Anstice's new home, at some unspecified distance from Penrith. When Anstice wakes on the first morning, she is captivated by the beauty of what she finds around her.

> Such an exquisite view was before her. First a sloping green park with magnificent old spreading trees grouped here and there, under which cattle were browsing, then the blue lake like a sheet of glass lying between the purple Fells, which ranged themselves around it, in various heights and shapes, and with beautiful shadows passing to and fro.

Anstice's conquest of the children (and, ultimately, her husband) is both plausibly and pleasantly described. Her excursions on foot around the surrounding district bring many of the traditional Lakeland adventures. Meanwhile, Anstice realises that she has also embarked upon another quite different pilgrimage of her own, for as soon as she enters the quiet village church, she knows:

> She had never gained a real knowledge of her Lord as a personal Friend. And she felt now that she had children to teach and train and influence, that she must have something worth passing on.

Anstice with her adopted family

Penrith Station is also the starting point for a book in quite a different genre of writing for juveniles. This is **The Lakeland Mystery (96)** by Geoffrey Trease, published in 1937.

In this early work for children, Trease set out to create an old-fashioned mystery story. 'Snowed In' would be a good alternative title, for that is the premise of his creation of the 'locked-room' mystery. All the characters are confined to a Westmorland inn by a blizzard which falls during the period of the Christmas festivities. Most of the main detective fiction ingredients are to be found within these pages: a crime, a small set of characters who could have committed it, two young boys acting out the part of the sleuth, a stream of clues—including red herrings—and a dénouement in which everything is explained. Unfortunately, in its attempts to ape the murder mysteries for adults that were coming to the peak of their popularity in the 1930s, it becomes palpably false and just doesn't work.

The Lakeland Mystery is still an interesting read but gives only a few glimpses of Trease's later high quality Lakeland stories.

Animal Adventures to the South of Ullswater

Now we must press on beyond Penrith into territory which stretches as far as the Kirkstone Pass but which still allows us a glimpse back at the M6 motorway and the famous rail line to the north. ***Hunter of Harter Fell* (97)** by Joseph E Chipperfield, published in 1976, is, at its simplest level, the tale of a lost dog that eventually gets found.

'Hunter' is the name of the Alsatian dog in the story and the 'Harter Fell' (there are two in the Lake District!) is the one not far from Hawes Water. Joseph Chipperfield was a prolific writer of animal stories for children and for many years shared his own life with an Alsatian. That he was inspired by the country in between the M6 to the east and the Kirkstone Pass to the west is conveyed clearly in his afterword, which declares that the story of Hunter was planned at Patterdale, near Ullswater in the Lake District. The geographical locations are very specific, as Hunter and the children who come to his aid cover a large area of mountainous terrain on foot in the early spring of the year. Margaret and Jimmie live near Rosgill, a community isolated in the lonely countryside yet within sight of the motorway and the main north-south railway. There are scenes set near the inn on the Kirkstone Pass, but also near the Abbey at Shap and the small community at Keld.

The book is a resounding endorsement of the superb qualities of the German Shepherd dog, its value as a working dog and its virtues as a family pet. However, it is also an exciting adventure story where the author catches well the sheer fatigue of walking endlessly across the upland countryside.

While we are exploring the rugged countryside to the south of Ullswater, it is an appropriate time to consider two stories about foxes, which have been designed to have a strong appeal for young readers. These are ***Lakeland Gray* (98)** by Richard Clapham, published in 1947, and ***Vix* (99)** by A Windsor-Richards, published in 1960.

There are so many similarities between the two books that inevitably, not unlike two foxes in the same territory, the trails of the two authors are destined to cross. Both are a delight to read and totally convincing in their detail.

Neither book is merely an account of the doings of the animals at the centre of the narrative. The whole world of wild Lakeland nature is reflected in their pages. The rhythm of the seasons, the habits and habitats of the other creatures that share this world, and the vital intervention of mankind are traced in convincing detail. Both authors are ably supported by the accomplished work of the illustrators with whom they have collaborated. The famous 'BB' or D Watkins-Pitchford was responsible for the many pictures in *Vix*, while Joan Rickarby brings to life the varied striking scenes in *Lakeland Gray*.

Both men demonstrate clearly a healthy respect for, and understanding of, the wild creature who is the farmer's inevitable adversary. For A Windsor-Richards it is 'glorious, untamed countryside', and he specifies no particular location for the scenes in the early years of Vix's life. Richard Clapham is more exact about Lakeland Gray's domain:

> On the east side of Gray's home dale, an ancient road led to the tops. It was the High Street of the Romans, along which they travelled from Windermere to Carlisle …

Both men, however, have taken the readers with them into the world of the fox—to the hidden crannies on the high fells where young cubs bask in the sunshine, to the labyrinthine earths beneath waterfalls and in old quarries where hounds chase in vain and terriers cannot force their way through to complete their part in the inexorable pattern of nature.

The Meaning of the Mountains—Helvellyn Once More
The same pattern of nature can be seen in the world of adults. In particular, what happens to us in our youth can have a strong formative influence on our future life and our ways of thinking. As we move up on to the slopes of Helvellyn once again, we come across another narrative by Bruce Carter (real name Richard Hough) whom we first encountered in *B Flight* (62). Once again, it is the life of a fighter pilot that is unfolded in this 1981 book, *Razor Eyes* (100). Hough makes his first person narrator, Mick Boyd, select two of his experiences whilst on holiday in the Lake District as defining moments in his life. In the story that follows their importance becomes clear.
    The first clarifies the uneasy relationship he has with his sister, Jo, and also identifies the principal traits in her character at this stage in her life.

> We were on Striding Edge, that knife-like ridge extending from near the summit of Helvellyn. It was bitterly cold and the four of us were huddled in the lee of a rock eating our sandwiches. I was feeling uneasy about the loose scree that fell away ever more steeply below us.

Mick clumsily drops the rucksack and it slides over fifty feet away until it stops. Nervously he contemplates going down to fetch it back.

> I could feel Jo's eyes on me. Her timing was perfect. Just when I thought I really thought I could do it—oh, yes, surely I could, taking it step by step— she called out, 'Oh, fooey!' and scree-ran down the fifty feet, sliding to a halt beside the rock, throwing the rucksack over her shoulder, and bringing it back.

The other Lake District incident in the book is the one that gives it the title of *Razor*

Striding Edge on Helvellyn in the foreground with Red Tarn clearly visible and, in the background, Ullswater (photographer: Peter Lewis)

Eyes. From the summit of Great Gable, the twelve-year-old Mick can see the top of Kirk Fell nearly a mile away. He also claims that he can see a fallen climber lying in a small crevice. This is something that neither his father nor his sister can pick out, but they agree to check if anyone is missing when they get down. Sure enough, a foolish lone climber is rescued because of young Mick's razor eyes. The razor eyes are to keep him safe on several dangerous missions during his time with Hurricanes and Typhoons.

Yet Another School and Another Cliff

'I'm frightfully glad our school is in the Lake District and not in some stuffy town.'

This declaration by Frieda in Phyllis Matthewman's ***Amanda at the Manor*** (**101**), published in 1954, sets both the scene and the tone for an absolutely standard girls' school story. It just happens to take place in a school called 'Felldale Manor' which is situated 'on the Patterdale side of Ullswater just outside the tiny village of Fellsdale'.

Unlike the other school story writers I have traced in this volume, this author operates on a very small canvas and completes her story within ninety-six pages. Although the

Manor School contains over one hundred pupils, only a set of about four middles, three prefects and two mistresses are introduced to the reader. Amanda is the new girl in the Lower Fourth, her sister Barbara is the new head girl, and Elspeth the new prefect who believes in a policy of strict punishment for even the most minor of crimes. Elspeth's obnoxious sense of 'rightness' alienates both the younger pupils and her fellow members of the Sixth Form. Unusually, the headmistress does not appear until page 94.

Against the System

Our last two stories in this section of the book take us back into the past once more and offer further glimpses of those characteristics that many authors see as having shaped the essential Cumbrian character. The first of these was written by Hester Burton, published in 1971, and is called **The Rebel** (102).

Frontispiece of *Amanda at the Manor*

Hester Burton once asserted that she wanted to show how ordinary people of the past were caught up in great events that have now become mere dates in history. In *The Rebel* she writes of an idealistic young man from Westmorland who finds himself somehow involved in some of the crucial incidents of the French Revolution.

The story begins on 5 November 1788 when all the Parkin family are making ready to celebrate one hundred years since the Glorious Revolution of 1688. The whole of Westmorland appears to be congregating in the town of Camberstock to pay tribute to the Duke of Ullswater, the local representative of the King. Stephen is the only man to stand out against what, for him, is a public show of subservience to a class of man whom he loathes.

Alas, Stephen is alone in his protest when he refuses to take off his hat as the Duke of Ullswater passes by. This earns him the anger of his uncles and the aggression of the drunken mob. The word 'democrat' is hurled at him as though it were the direst insult.

The author catches all the pent-up anger of Stephen's spirit as he argues with his uncles before they send him back to school:

> 'Why should I honour such a man?' Stephen was shouting.
> 'Because he is your better!' snarled Uncle Fletcher.
> 'Better! Do I beggar my tenants? Do I drive them out of their rightful homes?'
> 'Peace, you fool.'

'Do I pull a man's roof about his ears? And for what reason? Because I want his fields for my paddock! For my race-horses!'

Unfortunately for Stephen, his fate and that of his younger sister and brother lie in the hands of the uncles who have no sympathy at all with his revolutionary ideas. Stephen is to be sent to Oxford to complete his education, Josh is to be sent to sea and Catherine is to be sought a partner in marriage. How each one fares in the world is the plot of the rest of the book.

It is not until Josh travels home for Christmas that the journey through Ambleside, along the Kirkstone Pass and skirting the shores of Ullswater suggests that Penrith is the most likely model for Camberstock. Later, the proximity of the castle also indicates that Penrith is indeed at the centre of the hints. Similarly, the Ellenmere and Ellenhead where both Stephen and Josh attend school appear to be the lake and town of Coniston.

This moving book focuses for a long time on the fortunes of Stephen amidst the horror and chaos of France but actually achieves its central emotional attraction by a return to the lakes and the depiction of those around him, such as his sister Kate.

And so we return to the world of Peter Brownrigg, whose adventures were first encountered in *Cue for Treason* in our Keswick section (see page 115). Before we pass

Penrith Castle, near the railway station

Above: Ullswater steamer
Below: Ullswater from above the slopes of Helvellyn. Silver Point juts out into the
lake near to Norfolk Island (photographer: Peter Lewis)

on to Geoffrey Trease's next book, it is worth looking more closely at the events that take in some vital features of Ullswater. Kidnapped by the agents who are plotting the assassination of Queen Elizabeth I and who have already murdered his friend, young Peter awakes from unconsciousness to find his ears filled with the sound of water. There are four small islands at the southern end of the lake. The author does not reveal the name of the small one where the unlucky Peter is held prisoner for a while. My own reading of the text leads me to the conclusion that Norfolk Island is the one that Trease had in mind. When ruthless men cover all the roads, the only way to safety is to swim ashore and climb over the mountains. But where one boy can run, many men can follow. It's a long way to safety and an even longer way to London.

I urge you to take a trip on one of the motor vessels that regularly ply the lake during the summer months.

For nearly 150 years there has been a service carrying passengers round the various landings. From Pooley Bridge to Glenridding takes you from one end of the lake to the other. Many people use the Howtown pier halfway along to break their journey and complete the attractive scenic walk to Glenridding on foot. However, it is from the deck of one of the scheduled boats that you will get your best view of Peter's tiny island prison. You can stare at Norfolk Island and then imagine the desperate swim ashore to the small beaches that lie next to the Glenridding to Patterdale Road. As you glance at the fells above, you will get a true appreciation of the nightmare that faced him as his ruthless pursuers drove him before them up the slopes of Helvellyn.

To a certain extent Geoffrey Trease's **Silver Guard** (103), published in 1948, is a sequel to *Cue for Treason*. It uses the grown-up and middle-aged figures of Peter and Kit, the central protagonists of that Elizabethan adventure, as background characters in this story of the English Civil War. Once again, several crucial scenes are set on the banks of Ullswater where Silver Guard proves to be the name of the house that is Kit's family inheritance. Nevertheless, the central action of the book takes place in Oxford, where a young American, Gervase Steele, has come to study medicine regardless of the mighty conflict that is gradually engulfing the whole nation.

Gervase's arrival near Ullswater has not been without incident, for in the swirling mist on the mountainside he helped his newly found cousin Bell save her favourite sheep which had injured itself on the edge of a precipice. As the weeks of his visit to the Lake District unfold, before term starts at the university, he comes to delight in the company of his two cousins, Bell and Bob, and he learns that in the battles to come, their sympathies are more likely to be with Parliament than with the King. Gervase remains uncommitted to either side, determined to pursue his studies no matter what distractions come along.

By the latter stages of the book, the story has returned to the north once more, for

Silver Guard is under threat from Sir Richard Wickham, one of the Queen's messengers, who is busy helping to recruit a foreign army to invade and who has been promised the lands of the Brownrigg family as a reward for his secret missions to the French. When he attempts to claim Silver Guard by force, Kit organises the resistance of the local people until all the Brownriggs from the hills near Keswick arrive in force to drive him off in ignominious failure. The journey to fetch the family support is undertaken by Bell and Gervase by the light of the moon, and Geoffrey Trease gives a vivid and haunting account of their dangerous journey.

This is another book which celebrates the rugged independence of the Cumbrian people and the special quality of the countryside that bred them.

Silver Guard is a fictional house on the shores of Ullswater. Nevertheless, Trease gives certain clues as to its possible whereabouts. From the grounds of the house it was possible to see the island where Peter had his ordeal in the earlier book. A close study of a modern Ordnance Survey map tells us that the promontory jutting out nearest to the island on the southern side of the lake is called Silver Point.

Those who leave the motor vessel at Howtown can follow a well-defined path all the way along the coast past this viewpoint on the long trek to Glenridding. There is also a less arduous alternative. One of the guide books I have seen suggests that it is possible to park in Patterdale and to make a four-mile walk to Silver Point and back in about an hour and a half.

Just off the A592 on the northern side of the lake, nine or ten miles away from this fictional location, is a building which may have given the author some inspiration for the shape and feel of Kit's family mansion. Though not on the shores of Ullswater, Dalemain House contains behind its Georgian façade the elements of an Elizabethan manor house. It is in the interiors that you can seek for the atmosphere of Silver Guard. Particularly to be recommended are the winding passages, crooked stairways and half-concealed rooms. You can look round at the oak panelling and up at the sixteenth-century plaster ceiling. At this country house, the inevitable tea-room is in the medieval hall with its features dating back to the fifteenth century.

Our last look at Ullswater is destined to be a poignant one. The events of **Knights of the Sacred Blade** (18) and **Knights of the Lost Domain** (15) by Julian Atterton take us all over the north of England on both sides of the Pennines. The young hero, Simon de Falaise, is accompanied on each quest by Orm the Axe, one of the ancient community of Lakeland Norsemen who survived the incursion of the newcomers after the Norman Conquest and the reigns of the two Williams and King Henry. The stories are set during the troubled time of King Stephen, more than 800 years ago. A small Viking community

Behind the Georgian façade of Dalemain House you will find many of the elements of
an Elizabethan manor house.

survives at Longthwaite on the northern shore of Ullswater. It is the place that Orm
would call home, though he was banished from his native valley because of the killing
he made during a blood feud. The reader is allowed to witness the homecoming to his
brother after nineteen years out in the world.

It is in Longthwaite that Simon falls in love for the first time with the beautiful
Sigrid, Orm's niece. She is, however, promised to another, and Orm tells Simon that he
would do better to leave her untroubled by any thoughts of him. So Sigrid marries, and
when Simon returns it is to find that the beautiful settlement that he had come to
cherish so much has been attacked and the home of the Siggurdsons has been reduced
to 'blackened stumps'. Orm's brother, Orm's nephew and Sigrid's husband have been
seized and taken to Carlisle. To his horror, Simon realises that William Fitzduncan, the
man out to frustrate his quest for the Sacred Blade, has taken this action against
Longthwaite because of Simon's own involvement in the affair. He leaves behind the
lake like a 'silver serpent' and sets off to Carlisle. Carlisle itself is to present him with
the scenes of his greatest happiness and his greatest suffering: but you will need to
read *Knights of the Sacred Blade* and *Knights of the Lost Domain* to trace the rest of
this tremendous story. Meanwhile we must move on to a chapter containing, in three
versions, perhaps the best Lakeland story of all.

CRUMMOCK WATER AND BUTTERMERE

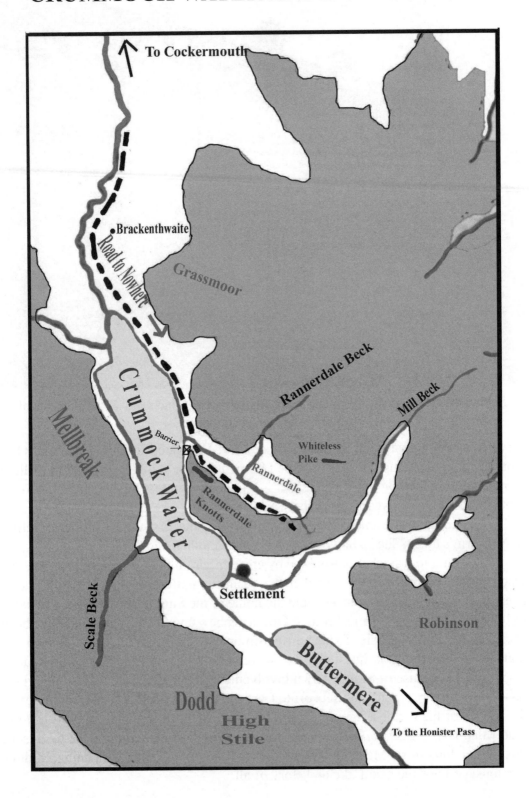

CHAPTER IX

IN THE SECRET HEART—DANGER AND SAFETY IN THE HIGH PLACES

Crummock Water, Buttermere, Rannerdale

SCAFELL PIKE, Scafell, Helvellyn, Ill Crag, Broad Crag, Skiddaw, Lower Man, Great End, Bow Fell and Great Gable. That's a roll-call of the ten highest peaks in England. They are all in Cumbria.

Of the hundred highest mountains in England, eighty-seven are in the county of Cumbria. It's at this point that you might begin to wonder why this particular part of north-west England is called the Lake District and not the Mountain District. Every year thousands of visitors set off to walk the high fells and face the challenge of the peaks. Some tackle individual routes as a part of a day's trip to the region. Others stay for longer, fascinated by the contradiction of such accessible remoteness.

In this chapter, we shall look at the books that deal with these mountains.

History, so the saying runs, is written by the victors. This seems to be particularly true of the Norman Conquest of England after the invasion of 1066. The single story that is retold in the last three books in this chapter springs from local traditions and legends. Rosemary Sutcliff points out the oddity of the fact that:

> Domesday Book, the Conqueror's Great Survey of England, stops short of the Cumberland fells, and Lake Land finds no mention in it.

What actually happened at this time near Crummock Water and Buttermere, the area marked in our final regional map, can never be known for certain. As we shall see, the peculiar geography of this mountain region and the skill of three dedicated authors can still bring alive the way of life of an earlier community who 'took to the hills' in a very different way from those seeking pleasure or thrilling challenges.

Before we come to them, however, we start with a personal crisis in the life of one young man.

> How long he had been sleeping when he had his nightmare he did not know. He awoke bathed in perspiration, and shaking in every limb … He did not sleep again. He watched the beams of white moonlight which filtered through gaps in the window curtains creep slowly along the floor, as the lady-of-the-night-sky swept through her orbit. He was sick with fear, for he knew that he dared not climb on the morrow.

This is the story of Scout Dick Goole in 'When the Devil Drives', another of the collection of tales called ***Adventurers, Ltd.*** **(10)** by Arthur Catherall.

If we look back over the children's stories already covered, we see a recurrent theme of dangers in the high hills. Each story of confrontation with the mountains is, to a greater or lesser extent, about finding yourself. In this last chapter of books that deal with specific places, I venture to suggest that certain authors have also attempted to take us to what they believe is the secret heart of the Lake District. On their way they have offered many clues as to what made the place and the people so special.

But before we go there, let us find out what happens to Dick Goole, who has for the first time to confront his fear of rock-climbing. He has all the correct equipment, and he has expert adult guides and supervisors to ensure his safety, but he just knows that he doesn't want to do it.

The day comes, and an accident happens just as he knew it would. Only the most extraordinary climb can save one of the instructors from certain death as he hangs in space with his rope fraying on the overhang above him. Dickie, out of sheer recklessness and terror, saves the situation by climbing 'Farquarson's Ginnel' and bringing the other instructors to the injured man's rescue. The 'Ginnel' is a route to the top of the crag which is avoided by even the most experienced climbers. As one of the other climbers declares: 'I suppose it was a case of "needs must when the devil drives", eh?'

A Climbing Holiday

A different sort of courage emerges in ***Peril in Lakeland*** **(104)** by Winifred Finlay, published in 1953.

Of all the Lakeland books in this selection, no other manages to visit so many of the high places. If, like young Dick Goole, you don't have the courage, the endurance or even the youth to climb Great Gable, Scafell Pike or cross the Sty Head Pass, then this is the children's book that will take you there.

The two girls, Gillian and Sally, have become good friends with Bryan and Peter, and, without any suggestion of romantic entanglements, enjoy spending their holiday time together, usually in the depths of the northern countryside. As Gillian and Sally live and go to day school in Leeds, whereas Bryan and Peter attend public school in Ambleside, this 'togetherness' for holidays is bound to strike the reader as slightly contrived. However, if we grant this initial premise, we must admit the author tries very hard to stick to real places and real emotions. Her one invention is a tiny fellside valley beneath the peak called Pillar.

Sally and Gillian prepare for their walking holiday with the boys by a short preliminary excursion up the Mosedale Beck, where they get themselves lost and meet old John Bowman, one of the last independent statesmen landowners of the Lake District.

For centuries his family have known no landlord, nor any local squire to whom they must pay respect or rent. He lives with his sheep and his sheepdog Ranger on his lonely stretch of land in Birkdale. Before he sets the girls back on the right path, they learn that modern civilisation has come to pose a threat to this lonely and beautiful valley. A visiting lawyer has arrived to convince him it would be better for him to sell his land, before the Government takes it over with a compulsory purchase order. Apparently it is the next section of the countryside to be sacrificed to the advance of the nuclear power industry. The girls promise to help John by consulting with friends of their parents about how he can resist this unwanted pressure to sell.

The next day Gillian and Sally meet the two boys outside their school in Ambleside and are introduced to Mr McGregor (Mac), the master who has promised to lead them on their expedition during the days of the half-term holiday. From this point onwards, the story tells of their walks and climbs between the different Youth Hostels in the region as Mac gradually breaks in his young charges to the pleasures and pains of the high places.

John Bowman, the lonely and independent Cumberland shepherd

There is much discussion of routes and walking methods, with descriptions of views and weather conditions, as the climate is both kind and unkind to the mountain novices during the succeeding days. A large part of the flavour of the book is created by the depiction of the characters they meet on the trail and at night in the Youth Hostels at Honister and Black Sail. With a few obvious exceptions, the climbers and walkers from all over Britain prove to be the salt of the earth.

Slowly the plot of the book makes its way back to the lonely Birkdale valley and the threat that appears to hang over old John Bowman. One evening, as the light draws to a close, an accident is reported to the warden of the Youth Hostel, and the good-natured camaraderie of the climbing and walking community hardens into something even more positive when each individual accepts a role in the team that is formed to go to the rescue. The climbers push themselves above and beyond the limits of endurance to ensure the injured man has a chance of recovery.

Whilst Mac is recovering from his efforts the following day, the four children set off to keep a rendezvous with John Bowman on the day that the lawyer is returning to renew his negotiations for the old man's land.

The ending of the book contains several surprises, not least a reversal in the assessment of the character of one of the earlier introduced characters. The reader is left wondering at the spirit of determination and independence that will allow the old Cumbrian, John Bowman, to face his future alone on the crags even though he is fully aware that his death cannot be very far ahead. The land he owns will be given to the National Trust so that his spirit, and the spirit of the place, can live on into the future.

Mountain Month (105) by Eric Mathieson, published in 1965, is more directly about climbing than any other of our Lakeland books. Johnnie Johnson is chosen by his school to go on an Outward Bound-type course in the Lake District. The clientele at Ghyll House are an interesting mix of characters and social types. The instructors are just as diverse, and just a little way down the valley is another group of tough, rebellious lads who are the cause of several conflicts and one hair-raising rescue under atrocious conditions. Without becoming appallingly technical, the author produces a convincing account of the methods and attitudes that are essential for successful and safe rock-climbing. The final episode in the book, the inevitable near-tragedy and emergency that is the ultimate proving ground of character, takes place near the slopes of Scafell.

Island on Crummock Water

One quick look at the map that heads this chapter will convince you that Crummock Water and Buttermere were once one bigger lake. Most travellers now visit them both in one day, stopping in Buttermere Village with its two inns, small car parks and access to the lake shores. Buttermere is a small lake which is hemmed in by various peaks and crags. The 'crooked lake' or Crummock Water is twice as long and half as deep again. At its foot lie the gentle flat-lands of Lorton Vale and the easy road to Cockermouth. Be warned that this same road, the B5289, when followed in the other direction, clings to the shore of the lakes for a while but then suddenly tackles the difficult steep and winding hairpin bends of the Honister Pass, which will eventually take you through the Jaws of Borrowdale down to Derwentwater and Keswick.

Three Versions of One Tremendous Story

At the end of this chapter's journey, we go back once again into the past and to the three books which both introduce and celebrate one of the most extraordinary series of events in the story of the Lake District. It would not be too fanciful to say that their story gives us the most complete and telling insight into the core of the Cumbrian character. The essentials of the tale of the Lakeland Norsemen's last resistance to the armies of William Rufus do not alter in the three books: *The Secret Fortress* (106), *The Shield Ring* (107), and *Falconsdale* (108). The very real Ranulf le Meschin, his brother William and King William Rufus appear in all three versions. Beyond the Honister Pass is believed to have been the secret fortress where the Scandinavian settlers of Lakeland held out against their Norman overlord—le Meschin. While the Vikings constantly raid any isolated road or coastal settlement, the Normans seek to destroy their homes. Peace negotiations near Ambleside are wrecked by the Normans slaughtering the Viking envoys. A horrible revenge is taken as the Viking defenders block and conceal the true road and then entice their enemy on to the killing ground that they have chosen. From the commanding heights of the surrounding fells they watch the Normans force their way into the trap of a narrow rock-ringed space from which there will be no escape—'the road to nowhere'.

The rest is folk tradition, legend and the survival of certain names in Cumbrian landmarks.

The three books are dealt with in the text that follows in the chronological order in which they were written. First comes *The Secret Fortress* (106), by Joyce Reason, published in 1946.

Joyce Reason's version begins in the dales of post-conquest north-west Yorkshire. The story is told by Osric Torfinnson, whose father was already a thane of the North Riding of Yorkshire and a great landowner round about Swaledale before the coming of William the Norman.

The book begins after a defeat at York, when some of the original landowners fled to Scotland and some crossed the hills into Cumberland. Osric's father clings on to the countryside in upper Swaledale, near Keld, where he is rarely bothered by the Normans. Later, after an abortive raid on Richmond Castle, the whole family is forced to flee to the possible sanctuary of 'Little Norway', which is run by Earl Boethar of the Mere, the man who eventually gives his name to Buttermere.

Osric has befriended Hakon, the brother of Earl Boethar, so his family are greeted favourably after they have made their epic journey through the helm wind. This extraordinary phenomenon is caused by supercooled air from the east rushing down the western slopes of the Pennines. After a period of calm weather, within a very few minutes the wind may be blowing so violently as to break down trees, overthrow haystacks, occasionally blow a person from his horse, or overturn a horse and cart. The refugees struggle first of all past the Rerecross on Stainmoor and over Cross Fell to Melmerby and thence to the secret fortress.

Pretty soon Osric is totally involved in the guerrilla tactics that have been used to keep the Normans at bay for so many years. Osric's friendship with Hakon grows, and his sisters begin to fit comfortably into the new world in the settlement by the lake.

Only his father, the old Earl, is discontented because his blindness means he can no longer contribute to the fight against the hated enemy. However, his chance for glory comes in a skirmish by the side of Windermere. Osric, with an injured man on his shoulder, is driven backwards to the edge of the water. He is ready to die rather than surrender in the face of overwhelming odds. Suddenly a whispering voice makes him look down under the low bank. There lies a boat, manned by his young boy servant, Dudda, and his own blind father. Happiness has returned to the old man because he can still play a useful part in the battle by using his immense strength to row the boat and save his son and his war companion. As he powers the boat to safety on the opposite side of the great lake, he is struck in the throat by a Norman arrow and dies, no longer a warrior but feeling like a man once more.

Elfwyn, Osric's sister

The constant defeats of their Norman adversary, le Meschin, have provoked his king, the notorious William the Red (William Rufus) to march north with a huge army. He arrives at Ambleside, and the men of Buttermere send a delegation to meet him, with the aim of negotiating a surrender. No matter how many times it is told, the story of the slaughter of the envoys still has the capacity to sicken the reader at the cowardice and brutality involved. Joyce Reason attributes the killing to the unreasoning anger of William Rufus and the treachery of a particularly nasty villain called Gilbert.

All their doubts about fighting have now gone, and Osric, Earl Boethar and Hakon make ready for one last glorious stand. Rufus marches out of Ambleside past Rydal and towards Grasmere. As though the judgement of heaven has fallen on them, the ranks of the enemy are overcome by the force of a suddenly descending helm wind. In panic they scatter back towards Ambleside but are picked off by the vengeful Northmen. Rufus and his barons barely escape with their lives. The traitor Gilbert is the only prisoner taken alive and, after questioning, his fate is certain.

The last section of *The Secret Fortress* concerns the trap of Rannerdale and the preparation of the killing grounds, details I will discuss when Rosemary Sutcliff introduces them in her later novel *The Shield Ring*. Joyce Reason's book ends with a description of how each member of Osric's family finds a future in the hills or on the sea beyond; and with a brief mention of the more honourable terms that Earl Boethar concludes with King Henry I and with le Meschin.

In ***The Shield Ring*** (107), published in 1956, Rosemary Sutcliff's vision of an eleventh-century Lake District is a harsh one. Only so gifted a writer could convince us of the terrible beauty of both the land and the people in the time of William II, and still leave us with the feeling that, even after hundreds of pages filled with slaughter, something worthwhile has been preserved. She sees it as the essential core of the region and of the people, a feeling of continuity with the past that is preserved in the present-day place names.

As with all the best stories, the book allows the reader to grow gradually into an understanding of the situation, and yet the life-or-death action begins on the first page. A reprisal raid for an attack on a Norman knight on the Lancaster road has destroyed Frytha's birthplace and caused the death of her mother and father. Grim the shepherd has saved the three- or four-year-old and carried her away northwards into the heart of the Cumberland fells. He heads for the stronghold of Jarl (a Scandinavian version of 'Earl') Buthar, the leader of the Norsemen, and turns the child over to the women of the royal hearth for them to nurture. However, the only one who can reach Frytha in her desperate fear is a boy called Bjorn, who is just a little older than herself. It is the relationship between these two young people as they grow to maturity that forms the backbone of the book.

All the men in Jarl Buthar's estate are fugitives. The Normans have gradually laid their heavy hands on the roads, towns and farmsteads that surround the inner redoubt of the Lake District. Like Frytha, Bjorn is an orphan, for his father has been killed fighting the Normans in Allerdale and his mother died soon after he was born. He is now foster son to Haethcyn, who had been his father's friend and who is the harper of the Jarlstead. The stronghold is at the foot of Crummock Water and the local stone-built chapel is at the head of Buttermere. These are secret places, so far never penetrated by the Normans who seek to bring all the land into subjection. Their method of doing so is to build forts and to drive forward the roads that lead north and south, and then east and west, across the Lake District. Jarl Buthar and his men contest every step of the way, and the years pass with not just the rhythm of the seasons, but with the more irregular pattern of attack, repulse, recovery and further attack.

It is against this background that Frytha and Bjorn grow up, revelling in the life in the high country, but well aware that danger and destruction can never be far away.

The war-band of Jarl Buthar grows ever weaker, while the Normans seem to have limitless supplies of men who will come across the seas in an attempt to put an end to this resistance. William II, referred to in this book as 'The Red King', is depicted as the harshest of enemies. Towards the beginning of the story, the Norsemen swallow their pride and agree to send a message to the Red King that they will bow their heads in fealty to him and consent to hold the Lake District under any Norman lord he names. Their greatest warrior, Ari Knudson, goes as messenger with a small band of companions. William has all the Norse peace-bringers slaughtered and their broken bodies set at the head of his army as battle standards. There can be no honourable peace settlement with such an implacable murderer.

As the stand-off turns into a battle by the side of Rydal Water, the Normans are defeated by two factors that they had not counted on. The first is the quite natural berserk anger that flows in the Norsemen when they see that the peace envoys have been treacherously butchered. The second is the helm wind, which blows in the face of King William's army. Routed and humiliated, the King and his army barely manage to escape to the old fort at Ambleside. Jarl Buthar knows that all further talk of submission is pointless; it will be a fight to extinction without any possibility of surrender. The Jarl still commands the stronghold but the leadership of the roaming war-band now passes to Aikin, who is determined to avenge the death of his foster father, Ari Knudson, with as much Norman blood as he can take.

The story of *The Shield Ring* takes in all of the Lake District, but Rosemary Sutcliff manages to create a special place in her readers' hearts for the inner stronghold near Crummock Water, where Bjorn and Frytha pass from their childhood into their teenage years amidst a community of men, women and children who are each brought to life as individuals. Bjorn grows in stature as a harper, but has doubts about how he will behave if he is ever put to torture. Would he be able to keep the secret of the stronghold if the fire began to bite into his flesh? His imagination makes him more gifted but also more vulnerable, and his apparent squeamishness makes him an enemy in the shape of one of the older boys called Erland, who casts aspersions on his courage. At the age of fifteen this precipitates his decision to seek his foster father's permission to join the war-band. Frytha, meanwhile, is also learning the ways of the warrior, for the Jarl knows that one day the future of their lives together may depend upon the resilience of the men and the women.

Bjorn proves his courage in a series of adventures. He fights with the war-band on Hardknott Pass and succeeds as a spy in coastal Workington. It is he who brings back the news of the planned raid by the Normans from the

A Norman attacked by arrows

unexpected direction of the north. It is this which leads to the preparation of the 'road to nowhere' as the Norsemen allocate their own area of killing ground if the worst should ever happen. When Ranulf le Meschin decides on a desperate throw of the dice with the biggest army he has ever assembled, Bjorn sets out on a final scouting expedition to establish the numbers of the enemy force. Frytha knows it is her destiny to go with him. They go down to Ravenglass and manage to win their way on to a ship to Workington and pass into the heart of the enemy army. An unlucky recognition leads to his exposure, and he faces the torture that he has dreaded all his life. Frytha too is captured and realises that Bjorn will never tell no matter what happens to either of them.

William Rufus, the Red King

A night attack on the Norman camp gives them the opportunity to escape and rejoin their people. The largest army ever assembled begins to makes its way southwards towards the secret stronghold. Another study of the map at the beginning of the chapter makes the course of events more clear. The constantly attacking Norsemen take a terrific toll on the Normans as le Meschin's army forces its way through to the lakeside of Crummock Water. However, these attacks are mere feints to draw the enemy army ever onwards until they see the mouth of Rannerdale opening to their left before them and think that their goal is in sight. The Normans believe that they have found the hidden valley and will soon be destroying forever the home of their enemies. How can they know that the real road has been blocked and that earthen banks and transplanted trees and bushes are diverting them up into a deadly ambush? Why should they think that the small band of men who fight so anxiously and flee before them are doing anything other than trying desperately to prevent them from reaching the houses where they keep their loved ones?

Before the Normans understand what has happened, they have ridden into Rannerdale, and the trap closes behind them as hidden warriors come round Hause Point and land from small boats to cut off their retreat. The slopes above the invaders are soon swarming with the warriors, and the killing begins, with the closely packed Norman knights unable to manoeuvre or resist the attacks of the first wave of berserkers, who sweep under the horses and stab upwards into their bellies. The air is filled with arrows that plunge down from the birch woods and take a terrible toll.

A once-proud army is reduced to a desperate rabble and the last battle of Lakeland has been won. Bjorn, though badly injured by the torture, has played his part and

Looking down Rannerdale to Crummock Water (photographer: Peter Lewis)

Erland, the man who once doubted him, has stood shoulder to shoulder with him as his shield bearer. Frytha has riddled the sky with arrows that rained down on the trapped Normans. Aikin has died in this battle, paying back in kind for the death of his foster father, and is buried, with his sword Wave-flame in his hand, on the hill that today bears his name.

For Bjorn and Frytha it is the end of a great adventure, for soon the community of the stronghold will disperse, returning to farm again in the lower valleys. But as they prepare to return to Bjorn's abandoned family farm in Eskdale, they know they are but starting on a new adventure.

And what is the shield ring that makes the title of this book? By the end of the book the reader has realised that it can be many things. It is of course the high barrier of the fells which prevents the Normans from breaking through. It is also the spirit of determination that inspires the Norseman to hold out against overwhelming odds. It is the trust that each man has in his comrades that, even if taken and tortured, no one will ever betray the secret places which mean so much. On the personal level, it is the dolphin ring that has come down to Bjorn from his ancestors, perhaps from the very people who built the ancient roads and fought over the ground that he thinks of as home. Bjorn leaves the ring with Frytha as he goes to the final battle, and she returns it to him as a symbol of their union. To those who have read Sutcliff's other books, it is a link to the other heroes, Roman, Celtic and Saxon, who have carried such tokens on their adventures. Whether the events in this story ever happened or not, this is Sutcliff's own attempt to link us with those northern people who have gone before and who have left us little else but legends and a few unusual place names.

Last of all we turn to **Falconsdale (108)** by Howard Jones, published in 1973 with a fine cover illustration by Douglas Phillips. Of the three accounts of the Northmen's resistance to the Norman Conquest, this is the shortest, the most bitter and perhaps the least satisfactory version.

Most of the action lies outside the Lake District itself, for the narrative of the book strays away from the description of the way of life of the small community and focuses on the life and adventures of young Alan and his desire for revenge on William Rufus. The author takes the dramatic step of making him present at one of the most significant events in the history of the English monarchy—the slaying of William Rufus in the New Forest.

For Alan, brought up on the high fells to be the guardian of the sheep, and expected to enter the church as a monk, the story of the slaughter of the envoys at Ambleside becomes a very personal matter. Both his father and his brother were amongst the ones tortured and killed because of the Red King's wrath. His pain, anger and confusion are made all the more vivid because he had actually made his way into the enemy camp and witnessed what happened. When he returns to the settlement by Buttermere, he begs the Earl (called the Falcon in this version of the story) not to send him to a monastery but to allow him to return to the sheep. For the rest of his boyhood he guards the sheep and trains himself to be proficient with the longbow. Little by little he realises what the dales and mountains mean to him:

> I loved them in all their moods; gay in the springtime with the gorse like golden fire above the bluebell mists; gentle in summer, with the hills immense and close, and the calm lakes glittering, and bees humming in the heather; mysterious in autumn when the peaks are remote and dreaming in the clouds; majestic and savage in winter whiteness with the north wind crying in the crags.

Eventually the day comes when the Falcon chooses him to go to Winchester to try to find out what plans the Normans have for attacking the Northmen once more. First, however, he must visit the Fens to see if those others fighting for the old liberties can offer any help. It is in this long excursion to the south that the narrative loses its power of conviction and dispels any sense of a possible reality as the young man has a series of adventures and escapes that would put Robin Hood to shame.

The return to the north and the exposure of the man who has betrayed all their secrets to the Normans revitalises the plot, and, as each man of Buttermere gets ready for the final encounter, the essential details of the trap exert their subtle grip over the reader once more. Howard Jones may call the place of slaughter Longdale instead of Rannerdale, but the familiar patterns of the conflict are closely observed:

> The path of retreat was blocked. They surged forward in panic. In panic they surged back. Some fought wildly with one another, some attempted to climb the steep slopes of Hagfell. Our men swept down on them in wave after wave.
>
> There never had been such a killing.

The book ends with an assessment of Henry I and the chances of reconciliation between the different races in England; and with, of course, the age-old story of Alan choosing for his wife the girl who has been destined for him since the first moment they met.

 Your own venture to the fells need not be so dramatic. A circular walk is possible round Buttermere in about two hours. Alternatively, you may follow a slightly more demanding but interesting route into Rannerdale, which involves a distance of about two and a half miles and an ascent of 850 feet. From the small car park at Hause Point on the B5289 take a short but straightforward climb to the top of Rannerdale Knotts. A green path leads steeply up to the ridge, and rocky crags are soon visible above you. A recently restored path to the left takes you directly through the crags and out on to an easy grass walk with a few rocky patches to the summit. Crummock Water and the distant Lowes Water can be seen to the north. Buttermere and the High Stile ranges can be seen to the south.

To make the descent into Rannerdale you must follow the ridge until you can begin to see the Buttermere to Newlands minor road. You will soon spot the saddle below you to the left where the path up to Whiteless Pike emerges from the valley lower down. You need to curve back round to the descent. It has a reasonable gradient and there is good grass underneath your feet.

You are now looking down on to the place where the Normans were lured to their destruction. Over a thousand years the landscape has hardly changed at all, and yet it is difficult to imagine a quieter valley than Rannerdale nowadays. A visit in spring gives you the opportunity to view the hosts of bluebells which cover the slopes and which local legend suggests mark the place of the slaughter. To complete the journey and the experience, carry on to the foot of Rannerdale. Follow the path to your left that takes you round the foot of the fell and back to Hause Point. And now you must think what effort it would have taken to block the road, disguise its existence and thus conceal the fact that a hidden fortress lay beyond.

If you read just one of the three stories then my recommendation is for *The Shield Ring*. It will be the easiest to find and it provides the most haunting of memories.

We must not forget that other writers in this book have caught the echoes of this story. Winifred Mantle shows us a family imitating the Northmen and retreating from a wicked villain to their own version of sanctuary in *The Hiding Place* (see page 104). In *Cue for Treason* (see page 115), Peter Brownrigg's father and his neighbours throw down the enclosure wall erected by the outsider who wants to add to his land.

> We weren't gentry, we were yeomen—'statesmen' or 'estatesmen' we call ourselves up here—but we were independent people, nor caring much for man or devil.

At the end of Trease's book the favour that Peter asks of the Queen is for her to confirm the tradition that the local Cumbrian families should be allowed to hold on to the common land. He says:

> 'We have farmed our fells, and held our land against all comers, asking no favours.'

The idea of the 'estatesmen' persists in the character of John Bowman whom we met earlier in this chapter in *Peril in Lakeland*. I like to think that the writers of the last three books in this section have all taken their own opportunity to bring alive a vague legend and to turn it into the legacy of an exciting and moving story.

What then remains?

We have covered each section of the Lake District. We may have even penetrated to the secret heart. Has the journey ended? The final stage of our pilgrimage must take us on to encounter those children's stories which claim a Cumbrian pedigree without giving us a real place from which to begin. The surprise is that they too can offer us excitement, variety and even a sense of deep fulfilment.

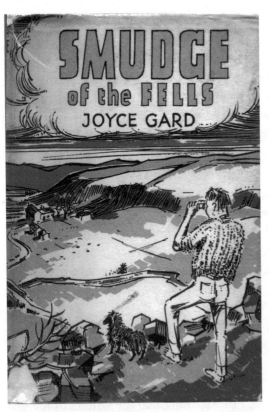

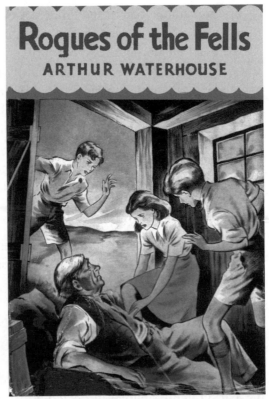

CHAPTER X

ANYWHERE, EVERYWHERE, NOWHERE
Unspecified locations in Cumbria and the Lake District

THE Normans who were slaughtered at Rannerdale were deliberately led on to a 'road to nowhere'. Now we ourselves move into some uncharted territory and hope that our fate will be kinder.

No map will do for this section of this guide, for this chapter deals with the books that have no specific location, and with those stories which are so deeply rooted in fantasy that the mentions of real settings are of little importance. Furthermore, no list of 'other' Lakeland, Cumbrian or North Lancashire books can hope to be all inclusive. This is a journey without an ending. In terms of content, more stories are mentioned in this last section, though fewer are dealt with in any depth.

Alphabetically first in our list of the remaining authors, Ruth M Arthur, with her *The Little Dark Thorn* (109), published in 1971, also illustrates well some of the problems associated with trying to 'place' the children's stories which have scenes in the Lake District. In some cases, there are just no answers to the questions. Yet strangely enough, Ruth M Arthur, like many of the other authors who do not identify specific landscapes, manages to create enough genuine atmosphere to make the setting feel truly authentic.

The story of *The Little Dark Thorn* concerns the growth to maturity of Merrie, the daughter of an English man and a Malaysian woman. With the onset of trouble with the Communists, 'raids, ambushes, shootings, burnings', Merrie's father decides to return to England, taking his six-year-old daughter with him. Merrie is filled with both fear and resentment at being wrested away from her mother. She seems to have nothing in common with her father, not even the colour of her skin.

Intent both upon earning a living and pursuing a career that involves further globe-trotting, her father leaves her with his relations in the Lake District. Abandoned at the home of her Aunt Emma, it takes Merrie a long time to adjust to her new environment. The story is told in the first person, and the author succeeds in maintaining the child's viewpoint by showing how the world gradually expands from Great-Aunt Emma's house, with her cat and dog, to include the streets of the nearest (unnamed) market town and then the nearby river and fells. Merrie has to come slowly to terms with the people and places she lives among. The author cleverly uses the child's first experience of snow to reflect both her wonder and her misery. She carries some carefully into the house, but later her delight turns to anger and distress as it melts to a dirty puddle of water. She reflects then on the way of the world:

'I cried because my beautiful snow was gone, and because nothing lovely ever lasted.'

The rest of her life maintains this pattern of finding something that eases her loneliness and gives her hope, followed by the sharp introduction of some greater tragedy. Merrie may be only six when the story begins but this is not a book for young children.

Back with the Boy Scouts

On several occasions during earlier chapters in this book we have been taken by Arthur Catherall into the world of the Boy Scouts as envisaged back in the 1940s and 1950s. *The Bull Patrol* (110), published in 1941, and *Adventurers, Ltd.* (10) contain stories which are all set in a territory loosely called 'The North of England', though it takes little imagination to see that many of the boys' adventures are meant to happen in Lakeland.

In each book, the basic premise is that a group of boys form a new Scout patrol. The boys in *The Bull Patrol* get together after a period of hostility caused by a dispute over a camping place. The lone Scout, Jim Barnes, convinces four others to join him in a special patrol after they have shared in an exciting encounter with a bad-tempered bull and an equally bad-tempered farmer. The other stories in the book take the boys into many different sorts of escapades. The leading characters keep varying, as Catherall brings out the different personalities of each of the members. Two of the themes that predominate are those of courage and honesty. There is also constant allusion to the difficulties of recognising the narrow line between bravery and foolhardiness or lack of care for others.

The last story in the book, 'Paying the Piper', brings together two Lakeland themes that we find elsewhere in children's literature. The first concerns hunting. Dick Henshaw is left on his own whilst the rest of the patrol departs to find more materials to rebuild the bridge on Farmer Birkett's land. A fox, which is being pursued by the hounds, arrives at the river bank to find his usual route to safety gone. Dick, taking pity, makes up his mind to put a temporary structure in place and to remove it again before the hounds can catch up. The fox scuttles across to freedom, and very soon the hounds arrive, to be frustrated. Dick meanwhile has hidden himself, but the rest of the patrol arrives to receive the anger of the frustrated huntsmen. The denials of his comrades are dismissed as lies as the hounds discover the scent of the escaped fox on the temporary bridge structure. As the Master of the Hunt says: 'I don't mind your being kind to animals ... but I do hate a liar.'

Unwittingly Dick has plunged the reputation of the local Scouts to an all-time low. The Bull Patrol is to be reported to the local Scout Commissioner as a rotten one. The second Lakeland theme emerges when Dick and the patrol redeem themselves by their behaviour when a small aeroplane drops out of the sky on to a lonely farm. In particular, their actions reverse the opinion of the Master of the Hunt, who has suddenly realised for himself the courage it takes to 'face the music'.

Without doubt, each tale has a moral, which is usually explicitly stated but which doesn't diminish the author's power of description, nor the inventiveness of his plotting. The Lake District references may be shadowy but there is no doubt that he was a writer who, on many occasions, was capable of promoting a convincing Cumbrian atmosphere.

Horror Comes to Cumbria

Towards the end of the junior horror novel **Buzzbugs (111)**, by Richard Hough writing as Bruce Carter, which was published in 1977, there is a newspaper article purporting to come from the *West Cumbrian Mail*. It contains the startling sentence:

> A large area of west Cumbria has been placed under martial law by order of the Chief Constable of the County, and a statement from Emergency Military HQ in Barrow states that all traffic movement in an area bounded by a line between Whitehaven, Buttermere, Hawkshead and Broughton in Furness is subject to military control.

By this stage in this exciting story, the tale of two children and the problems they

The river flowing from Buttermere towards Crummock Water

face in the lonely Lakeland valley of Millbeck has developed into a wider story of national and international significance. Part of the success of the book is contained in the way the author keeps a balance between the purely domestic affairs of John and Lucy, and an almost forensic investigation about how the 'Buzzbugs' of the title come into existence. With great skill, Bruce Carter engages the readers' feelings by a cunning comparison of a repellent human being and a horrifying threat from the insect world.

The human being is the repulsive Mrs Effingham, a breeder of thoroughbred horses. Her tendency to resort to the law, and her brutal and hectoring manner, give the lie to any tradition of friendliness amongst the folk of Cumbria. It goes without saying that she is an 'offcomer' or outsider but, as John realises, she is a woman determined to have her own way and capable of humiliating his father and driving the poor farmer to the brink of despair.

The first raids by the newly hatched bugs give some hint of the horror that is to come. The Buzzbugs are formidable in size, and they kill their victims by landing on them and inserting a proboscis to suck out the blood. A group of escaped horses provide easy prey, for they panic at the sight of the creatures, trip and break their legs. Both John and Lucy realise that they must tell the world of the danger when they witness a mare in foal being sucked dry before their eyes.

The easy route for the author is then not taken. John and Lucy do *not* save Mrs Effingham's life and become reconciled to her by fighting the common danger from the creatures. Instead she is chased in her car, the V8 engine of the Jensen driving the vehicle faster and faster away from the menace that pursues her. On the straight sections of road it looks as if she is winning but the insect nemesis cuts across the bends, and suddenly: 'Car and insect were as one.'

Mercifully for Lucy, a sudden squall makes it impossible for her to see what happens next. Reports of human deaths elsewhere in the valley have already started to come in, and both the police and the military have begun to take action. In a satisfying conclusion, the story is brought full circle when the stomach-churning invasion is ended by the imaginative response of the young girl. I will end by asserting that of all the people you are likely to meet in a journey through children's literature, Mrs Effingham will prove to be one of the most satisfyingly awful villains.

Much more well known than *Buzzbugs* is **Urn Burial (112)**, by Carnegie Medal-winning author Robert Westall, published in 1987. An eighteen-year-old shepherd works on the fells to the north of the Lake District. All around Ralph the world of the traditional fells is changing. He rides across the slopes on a scrambler bike and follows the thin wire line of the fence towards the summit of Fiend's Fell. The old stone walls that provided winter protection for the sheep are now gone. His conclusions about the ruthlessly modern and reordered landscape are totally depressing: 'Everything was getting spoiled these days.' Yet it is not until he digs into a cairn of stones and discovers a strange sleeping creature that the world really changes. The horror that follows is grim and unrelenting. Before he knows it, Ralph has awakened a dangerous and terrifying secret that spells tragedy for the whole of mankind.

Keswick Station

The Ghosts of Ravens Crag **(113)** by Hugh Scott, published in 1996, is another dark supernatural mystery which uses the Lakeland landscape as the setting for the horrific ordeal of an ordinary family. There's a lake, an island, an old church, a haunted tarn, a suspicious bridge and a host of malevolent ravens. Once again, however, the reader will search in vain for the real places that inspired the events of this tale.

The Public School Story
Our most complete picture of relatively modern school life comes in Geoffrey Trease's Bannermere stories, but the traditional 'Golden Age' English public school story is also represented by the doyen of boys' school story writers—Talbot Baines Reed. Strange to note, the author of ***The Cock House at Fellsgarth*** **(114)**, published in 1893 in book form, was always a day-boy, unlike the majority of his heroes and villains.

The Cock House at Fellsgarth is almost certainly meant to be set in the Lake District, but it is better to acknowledge immediately that the landscape he creates is a purely imaginary one.

> Not know Fellsgarth? Have you never been on Hawkswater, then, with its lonely island, and the grey screes swooping down into the clear water?

And have you never seen Hawk's Pike, which frowns in on the fellows
through the dormitory window?

So far, a nice, typical Lakeland evocation; it could even (except for the island) be a
picture of Wast Water. However, in the next sentences Reed adds in details about Hawk's
Pike that seem more to conjure up a school set in an Alpine valley:

I don't ask if you have been up it. Only three persons, to my knowledge
(guides and natives of course excepted), have done that. Yorke was one,
Mr Stratton was another, and the other—but that's to be part of my story.

It may safely be said that if you decided to read only one public school story of the
last quarter of the nineteenth century, then *The Cock House at Fellsgarth* would be a
remarkably good choice. It is full of energy, good humour, well-crafted plotting and an
attractive narrative voice. The religious ethic is there, but implicit in the behaviour of
the characters, and at no time is one subjected to moralising or preaching in order to
ram the message home.

Music in the Mountains

A most extraordinary book for younger children is ***The Concert by the Lake*** (115) by
Rebe P Taylor, published in 1960. It stands out from all the others in the Lake District
collection because of the author's almost overwhelming concentration on the *sounds*

of the countryside. The opening is conventional, with
young Angela disappointed at finding that she has to
spend her spring holiday in Aunt Becky's cottage in
the Lake District rather than going to Switzerland.
Moreover, she finds that she has to consider herself in
charge of Jeremy, her irrepressible eight-year-old
brother.

On her first walk with local lad Tom, she discovers
that there is a lot about Westmorland that she needs to
learn.

'Look at these walls, for instance. They're drystone walls—fitted together like a jigsaw puzzle,
without a scrap of mortar, ten feet high
sometimes. You won't find walls like that
everywhere, you know!'

Under Tom's guidance, Angela is quickly won over, yet it is not just the beauties of
nature that she can see—the bursting out of yellow pussy-willow, the spring of a squirrel
over her head and the long streak of unmelted snow on the horizon—which have the

most dramatic effect on her. It is lonely Paul from the stone mansion called Thicket Grange, who enchants them all by the power of the music that he gets them to create. Immensely talented in his own right, Paul also has the capacity to lead the others, even the ebullient Jeremy, into wanting to make harmonies which are in perfect tune with the surrounding countryside. The result is a magical, almost idyllic, representation of country life that, when played at the concert in a special setting by the lakeside, wins the approval of both the locals and the people who have come as visitors to the area.

Less successful is *Hilary's Island* (116) by Elinor Lyon, published in 1948. It may not even be set in the Lake District, and it is decidedly an odd book even by the standards of some of the others in this last section. The story is set near a lake and apparently in the north of England. The plot, involving the escapades of a girl who is not what her aunts believe her to be, is just as enigmatic as the setting. Much of the action depends upon an implausible impersonation which suggests that the adults in the story are either extremely short sighted or just plain stupid. The author would later write many more successful and more convincing stories for children.

Lots of Books for Younger Children

And now it is time to take a quick gallop through some of the more recent children's books, usually for the under-twelve age group, which have used the Lake District as a background.

The first of these is not so much a book as a phenomenon. From the point of view of quantity, it is very satisfying to deal with over thirty children's books in one go. The Home Farm Twins series by Jenny Oldfield has been produced by Hodder Children's Books from 1996 onwards. While it may take a while to collect all of these 120–122 page adventures, they are so readily available in bookshops and libraries that it would be unfair to give anything more than a brief picture of what they contain.

Once again we are 'somewhere' in the Lake District. The local villages, towns and farms are all given names that betray their fictional identity. There is a lake called Doveton Lake, and a café, where the twins' mother works, called the Curlew Café, in Nesfield. Hannah and Helen live in a world that is made secure by their loving parents and interesting because of their overwhelming desire to start owning and caring for creatures of all sorts. The series starts with *Speckle the Stray* (117), which was inspired by the author's own dog, called Tess. Later adventures include the story of a day spent helping out at a cat sanctuary in *Mitch Goes Missing* (118) and checking up on a Dalmatian that appears to be neglected by its owner in *Spot the Prisoner* (119). It is no surprise when they start looking after the piglet runt at the neighbouring farm in *Sunny the Hero* (120). These are warm, friendly books which offer a positive picture of family life and a world full of animals.

The attractiveness of animal stories for young readers is brought out again in *Labrador on the Lawn* (121) by Lucy Daniels, published in 2003. This tells of the experiences of Mandy and James, who are staying at a holiday cottage in the Lake District when they spot a mischievous Labrador. James's dog Blackie is delighted to have found a friend, but with no identification or collar, how will they find her owner?

The Snow Dog (**Puppy Patrol**) (**122**) by Jenny Dale, published in 1999, is the twenty-sixth book in another series based around the busy King Street Kennels. In this story, the owners' children, Neil, Emily and Sarah, have adventures in the snowy Lake District, with a spaniel pup named Princess.

In the Jackie series by Judith M Berrisford, horses rather than dogs were at the centre of the young girl's concerns. In one adventure, *Jackie and the Phantom Ponies* (**123**), published in 1979, Jackie and Babs arrive to spend their holidays on David Browning's stud farm in the Lake District and soon find they have a mystery on their hands.

Whilst we are engaged in this exploration of stories for young children, it is time to take a further step down the age ladder and talk about one of the superstars of young children's picture books. This is the legendary *Postman Pat* (**124**), the star of John Cunliffe's many books which began in 1980, and the doughty public servant of the fictional and idyllic Greendale. John Cunliffe has admitted that many influences came together in the creation of the people and the places which later became so famous. Early experience with the Northumberland mobile library service, thirty years before he began to formulate that special world, sowed the seeds of his liking and respect for those who lived in remote rural environments. However, it was during his time living near Kendal that he began to make contact with the people who were his neighbours in the streets of Greenside, on the outskirts of Kendal. He chatted with the man in the local post office and a local teacher who introduced him to her many friendly and hospitable friends in the farming community.

It is time also to mention *Scratch and Co* (**125**) by Molly Lefebure, published in 1968. With its subtitle *The Great Cat Expedition*, this tale turns out to be about an unusual attempt to climb the 'Highest Known Peak' (Scafell Pike). The author has her intrepid cats use rabbits and terriers as porters and, apparent to those in the know about the mountaineering world, also seems to use them to re-enact or parody some of the more famous disputes of those climbers who tackled the Himalayas. Lefebure's next book, *The Hunting of Wilberforce Pike* (**126**), published in 1970, is about many of the same bunch of cats, but is in fact a prequel detailing the long battle that they have with a notorious cat snatcher, Wilberforce Pike. He meets his fate by falling off Striding Edge into the mists above Red Tarn. The illustrations by the famous Alfred Wainwright add to the vividness of both adventures but can't quite rescue them from the world of fantasy.

I have deliberately separated *Flow* (**127**) by Pippa Goodhart, published in 1994, from the other younger children's books about animals because it is not part of a large, very commercially orientated series. Yet in a strange way it is linked with three of our other Lakeland stories, for it was runner-up for the Kathleen Fidler prize for children's literature. (You will remember that Kathleen Fidler gave us our first book, *Lanterns over the Lune*, as well as *The Droving Lad* and *The Deans to the Rescue*.) The story of Oliver in *Flow* is a moving one. Challenged by dyslexia, Oliver's performance at school is always disappointing. The author gives an admirable picture of a teacher who is not unkind, but just hasn't got the knowledge or the perception to see that the sensitive boy isn't merely lazy or stupid. The arrival of a head teacher who has a very personal instinctive understanding of his problems signals a brighter prospect for the future.

'There is trouble at Fellside Farm in the Lake District. This is a grand open-air adventure full of exciting characters.' So runs the publisher's blurb for *Rogues of the Fells* (129) by Arthur Waterhouse, the second in a series which began in 1948, and it can apply equally fairly to the complete trilogy. They were all written for seven- to ten-year-olds and they all concern the same group of three children and same small farm.

'The farm where the Wains lived was just off one of the lonely roads that wind in and out of the great hills in the Lake District.' That is as precise as it gets. Arthur Waterhouse never mentions a single real place, nor does he ever indicate just what particular section of the greater region the setting is meant to be. From the point of view of his young readers, what the stories are principally about is children, sheepdogs and sheep.

Raiders of the Fells (128) tells of how Harry and Tess Wain, together with their friend John Grayson, manage to frustrate the activities of a gang of sheep rustlers. In ninety-five pages and nine chapters they strive to round up the thieves, who tend rather foolishly to return to the scenes of their crimes the night of every full moon. Amongst the tactics used by the daring children are rugby tackles and the removal of a 'small object' from the engine of the thieves' van.

Rogues of the Fells (129) contains another favourite device, often used when juvenile writers are in sheep country. This is to develop the story of the renegade dog who has become a sheep worrier. You will not be surprised to learn that those 'darned' children prove too much for the law-breakers once again.

In some ways *Fly of the Fells* (130) is the most effective of the three books. Eric Knight's *Lassie Come Home*, with its story of a dog's incredible journey from Scotland to Yorkshire, is the most famous example of this theme of a lost dog seeking its owners. The story of Fly's disappearance draws upon some of the same features which made the Lassie story so appealing. Arthur Waterhouse's introduction to the Lake District is gentle, but one which is totally appropriate to his very young readers.

Fantasy Flying

One dream that many young children have is that suddenly and magically they can soar off into the sky and fly. That is the basic premise of *Woorroo* (131) by Joyce Gard, published in 1961.

Ten-year-old Mark Danby stumbles across a secret from the past that causes him to meet the strange wizened creature called Woorroo perched at the end of his bed one morning. Woorroo is one of the ancient bat people, condemned to longevity but blessed with the secret of flight, which, if he wants, he can share with the discerning young of a new generation.

With his father in India on government service, and his mother in the USA to pursue her career as a model, Mark is able to smuggle Woorroo to the lonely vale in the Lake District where he hopes he will be shown how to grow his own wings.

All the preparations take place, his wings are grown, and Mark glides into the air. The chapters unfold gradually, with him learning how to swoop over the lake and around the encompassing crags. In sunshine, in mist, and in heavy downpours, the young boy thrills to his new-found freedom. Woorroo proves to be not just the perfect flying companion but also a source of peculiar knowledge that allows him to talk to all the local birds.

Once you have accepted the basic concept, it is a pleasure to allow yourself to go where the winds and the author will take you. Much more difficult to grasp are the key elements in the world of the sequel, *The Dragon of the Hill* (132), published in 1963, which contains a confusing blend of legend, folklore and history.

The central element of the plot is the seizing of young Jenny by a dragon that appears to have its lair under, or rather inside, one of the surrounding mountains.

Events come to a climax on a lake island in the middle of the underground cavern. There, Jenny and the friends who seek her meet up with a sleeping figure, who, when roused, informs them that he is Brandreth Gawain, a lord of the Lakeland fells at the time of the Romans. From this point onwards, the author attempts to draw together all the different strands that she has spun to get her characters to this part of the story. The explanation involves the history of a conquered people, the meaning of the standing stones, the sacrifice of Gawain, the true role of the dragon and the introduction of an all-powerful and all-knowing Earth-mother.

In *Fell Trek* (133) by Marjorie Lloyd, published in 1973, we can see examples of the completely opposite sort of writing for children, for this story is deeply rooted in everyday reality. It tells of an interesting five days' tramp amongst the hills for the Fothergill family. One week in June, Mr Fothergill and his four children set off into the Lake District with Rubber, their dog. No locations are specified, and the reader is presented with friendly bed-and-breakfast landladies, even more friendly farmers and a mysterious duo who prove to be harmless despite all the children's wildest speculations. *Fell Trek* lacks that extraordinary feeling of place that the author captures so effortlessly in the earlier-mentioned Fell Farm stories and in her masterpiece *The Farm in Mallerstang.*

Crooks on the Fells
To the experienced reader of children's literature of the past, it comes as no surprise at all to encounter two books by Eric Leyland amongst the ones that are set somewhere in

the Lake District. The first we examine, **Rustlers of the Fells (134)**, published in 1960, is an eighty-four-page book in the Nelson Peerless series. It is a good example of the writing of this prolific author who had more than 300 children's books to his credit. Leyland's principal plot device, which admittedly he shares with many other writers, is to provide a surprise revelation in the last chapter. This nearly always follows the pattern of the obvious suspect being proved to be innocent and the person you least suspected being found to be guilty.

> His face was no longer pleasant but drawn in harsh, dangerous lines, the
> lips pulled back like an animal's.

You will notice that the name of the villain has been carefully excluded from this account. After all, this might be the only Leyland book that a reader ever comes across, and it would be bad sportsmanship to rob him or her of the main reward.

Leyland once described himself as a 'competent hack'. As some of his school stories deal well with character-led situations, this is really an unfair dismissal of his own talents. On this occasion, in *Rustlers of the Fells*, he produces a reasonably crafted story within the very special constraints placed upon him by the series editor.

At 221 pages, **Mystery Moor (135)**, published in 1950, is an even more substantial attempt by Eric Leyland to set one of his adventures in the Lake District.

The age group being targeted would appear to be older than that for *Rustlers of the Fells*, for the young protagonists are all about seventeen and in their last year of public school.

In an unusual twist, the standard gambits of sheep rustling, robberies from remote country houses, stealing of rare birds' eggs, kidnapping of important scientists, and so on are replaced by a grim reminder of our barbaric past. What is hidden in the quarry cave and what will take place on the quarry floor might seem pretty trivial compared with the big operations so beloved of children's adventure stories but for those who are appalled at animal cruelty it packs a strong emotional punch. What the crooks are organising is in fact a 'Mains', the name for a meeting for a series of illegal cockfights. In the end, Leyland makes the foiling of such cruel villains a very rewarding conclusion for any sensitive reader.

There was a great temptation to place *No Match for the Maitlands* **(136)** by Sheila L Mills, published in 1957, into the Penrith

Windermere (photograph: Adrianne Fitzpatrick)

section of this book. However, a re-examination of the text confirms that this would be appealing too much to a sense of neatness rather than clear-cut evidence.

In this story, the mother of the children who fall into adventure and solve the mystery is the manager of a hotel in the Lake District. The local town is called Moorfell and the only real location (apart from London) is Windermere.

With a skill worthy of Agatha Christie the author introduces a well-sustained red herring, and surely there is another nod to the mistress of crime when it turns out that the inevitable twins are called Pip and Emma after military slang—as happens in one of Christie's mysteries. Indeed, many of the stock characters of children's detective fiction make their appearance: the irascible professor, the red-faced policeman, the mysterious foreigner, the suspicious tramp, the reclusive writer, and the boy who fancies himself as a detective. This is an enjoyable 1950s children's mystery which could have happened anywhere.

Coming Home to Lakeland

As we approach the end of our fictional journey, it is appropriate once again to present a book which unravels many of the themes that have been celebrated in Lake District children's fiction. *Smudge of the Fells* **(137)** by Joyce Gard, published in 1965, is entirely different from the two fantasy fables by this author which I presented earlier in this chapter.

The story of a boy who runs away from an unhappy home to try to find a new way of life in the Lake District is, as we have seen, not that unusual. The theme of the cruelty of the wicked stepfather is also not a new one in children's literature. What makes Joyce Gard's story different from others of its type is that the home which poor Gerald seeks is laid out in the valley below him for so long, at times perplexingly within reach, and at other times seemingly unattainable.

In essence, the story passes through three stages. The misery and conflict of the first stage is summed up by the character of the awful stepfather whose name of Sid Pindle is reduced to the ever-threatening, monosyllabic, hateful nickname of 'Pin'. For Gerald and Pin, it had been hate at first sight, and it becomes clear that the stepfather's biggest ambition was to drive his new 'son' to tears on every possible occasion. The running away is developed as a natural consequence of such treatment, and an attempt by Gerald to recapture the happiness of the past holiday with his real father in the Lake District leads him to choose that particular area of the country as his sanctuary.

The second stage of the book is certainly the most captivating. In spite of its covering what can only be a transitional period in Gerald's life, it catches that restless feeling of something that isn't quite security and isn't quite peril. Gerald, with surprising ease, finds his way to a lonely valley where he is able to live with an old man called Lanty in his tumbledown shack near the entrance to a quarry. Gerald has found food and shelter, and a tenderness that he hadn't expected when he saves a small lamb from a storm on the fellside. Pretty soon the Smudge of the title becomes his inseparable pet. Some small jobs working in the garden for a local old lady provide him with the necessities of life. As winter turns to spring, Gerald finds himself climbing to the ridge on the mountains where he can look down into the next valley. With his binoculars he can watch and drink in every detail of the small farming community that lies below. It is a glimpse of forbidden happiness.

However, Gerald's life with Lanty proves to be increasingly precarious. The old man suffers from funny turns that could prove to be life-threatening. Worse than that, he has fallen into the hands of some villains from the towns, who are forcing him to run an illicit still producing moonshine alcohol. Worst of all, by an extraordinary coincidence vital to the plot, the boss behind the gang proves to be none other than Gerald's detested stepfather, Pin. On any of Pin's visits to the remote valley, Gerald knows that he might be recognised.

The resolution of the story provides the reader with two unlikely heroes. The first is the redoubtable Smudge, who is able to find his way across the many tracks of the hillside even when they are totally shrouded in mist. The second is Bryan Whiteside, the grown-up son of a local man, who is busy repairing long sections of the dry stone wall in the immediate neighbourhood. When Pin has Gerald tied up and at his mercy at the foot of a cave in the quarry, it is Bryan who cuts the boy free and who successfully contacts the local police. Gerald himself attempts to make his escape but runs straight into the arms of Pin. However, though all his former hatred of Pin persists, Gerald finds that his deep-set fear of the man has finally evaporated.

Gerald can fight and does fight, but it is pointless to resist a man with a gun. He begins to run through the underground caves, alert to the chasms that at any moment may appear at his feet. His awareness of this danger saves him—you will have guessed what eventually happens to his pursuer.

The third stage of the story is perhaps the most difficult for the reader to accept. The happiness described therein is just a little too idyllic to live effectively with the misery and the tension that have gone before. Happiness proves to be both a state of mind and the chance to live in the place one has come to know well during a time of danger. Gerald has come home to the Lake District.

The Lost Books, the Incomplete Journey and the Hidden Treasure

Both fortunately and unfortunately, we can never really come to the end of our journey to the children's books of Cumbria and the Lake District. A researcher can only hope that he or she has done justice to the material accumulated. However, this particular researcher would like to feel that there are still new (or old) books to be found. I already know that there are bound to be books that I have missed. There will surely be new books yet to be written.

It is fitting therefore that we should end with both the saddest and the happiest of these Cumbrian stories. On my quest through the shelves of second-hand books for relevant material, I came across a volume entitled *Quest for Romance* (138) by Frederick Cowles, published in 1947.

This is a collection of fables and legends linked by the character of the Story-Man who is portrayed as retelling them to the people of the towns he visits. One such story is 'The Outlaws of Englewood', which is based upon the events narrated in a famous 'Border Ballad'.

It tells of the doings of Adam Bell, William of Cloudeslee and Clym of Cleugh, the outlaws of the title. Even in summary form, it makes a marvellous tale and was, I thought, a narrative that deserved to be developed into a full-scale novel. Where else would you learn about the man who shot an apple off his son's head to demonstrate his prowess with the longbow to the King of England? (It is all the more remarkable because the story predates the deeds of William Tell.) Such a story cries out for a proper prose version.

One did once exist. In 1939, the Silloth author Patrick Barker had his manuscript for *The Outlaws of Inglewood* accepted, published and printed. The outbreak of the Second World War brought the paper shortage, and so all his efforts were pulped and only six copies were left. It has never been republished and it was only from his son that I learned this sad tale. A series of Cumbrian adventures to rival those of Robin Hood thus became a lost book.

All we can do now is stand under the great trees at Hutton in the Forest—all that now remains of the famous Inglewood (Englewood in the ballad)—and dream that one day some talented writer will turn 'The Merry Men' of Cumbria into a famous children's story.

I sing of Carlisle city
In merry days of old:
I sing of forest pathways,
I sing of outlaws bold.
They hunted there together,
Those men so brave and free—
Adam Bell and Clym of Cleugh
And William Cloudeslee.

In Englewood, fair forest,
When brightly gleams the dawn,
Is heard in ghostly echo
The music of the horn:
And down the years come riding
Those merry outlaws three—
Adam Bell and Clym of Cleugh
And William Cloudeslee.

The purpose of this book has been to lead you to stories and to look again at places that many know so well. Perhaps you can take the journeys in person. Perhaps you will revisit these scenes with an 'inward' eye as you tap once again into the imagination of so many different authors.

I make no apologies for ending the book where I began—with my own favourite children's author. Those who have read *The Gates of Bannerdale* by Geoffrey Trease will know exactly what he meant by its final words. I offer them again as my invitation to look afresh at this special part of England and the stories of the children's authors who can take you there:

'The treasure you seek longest is often close under your hand.'

Above: Windermere (photograph: Adrianne Fitzpatrick)
Below: The view to the platform at Lakeside station from across Lake Windermere in Fell Foot Park

POSTSCRIPT

THE UNFINISHED JOURNEY

THE author of any survey of children's books connected with a particular area must eventually call a halt to his enquiries if the manuscript is ever to move to publication. Previous experience with researches into the children's books of Newcastle and Northumberland has taught me that as soon as the finish line is drawn, something new (or old but previously undiscovered) will arrive to demonstrate that the journey will never really be over. So it has proved again.

I wasn't really surprised when another short tale by the super-prolific Eric Leyland was unearthed by me in the second-hand book market. *White Fury* **(139)**, published in 1956, is yet another story set on the generic Lakeland fells. This time he assigns the name Tarnmere to his particular creation, though there are views of Thirlmere and Ullswater to be enjoyed in the distance as Max and Scrap pursue the mystery of the walled house, the hermit who lives there and the wild creature that attacks the local sheep during the winter snows.

Another author who created many tales for children, set all over the world, (*Welsh Adventure, Caribbean Adventure, Paris Adventure* and so forth) was Viola Bayley. Amongst her least well-known and almost unobtainable books is *The Shadow on the Wall* **(140)**, published in 1958. A member of the Girlsown internet group, Margaret Walker, was kind enough to supply me with a short summary that gives the essential details. This adventure is set in an imaginary Westmorland village called Blay, which is situated somewhere 'south of Kendal'. The story concerns a group of four children and their twenty-one-year-old cousin Hattie, who inherits a guest house in the Lake District.

A much more serious omission from my original researches are the stories of Theodora Wilson Wilson. For my information on this author I am indebted to *The Encyclopaedia of Girls' School Stories* by Sue Sims and Hilary Clare. Theodora Wilson Wilson was born in Kendal in 1865 and many of her stories are set in her native region. Sims and Clare assert that her two school stories, *The Founders of Wat End School* **(141)**, published in 1932, and *The St. Berga Swimming Pool* **(142)**, published in 1939, have 'a strong sense of place'. They sum up her plots as follows:

> *The Founders of Wat End School* is perhaps more interesting, taking place in a recently established mixed boarding school, and focusing almost equally on the girls and the boys. Both stories use the standard discovery motif

(the discovery of a secret chamber in the first and medieval treasure in the second), but are lively books, if slightly stilted in style.

Theodora Wilson Wilson wrote many other children's books, some of which I have had the opportunity to read. ***Cousins in Camp* (143)**, published in 1914, is subtitled

A Lakeland Tale and thus would seem to fall within the remit of this study. However, though it is possible to suspect that Lancaster is the town which is the starting point of this story, it could just as easily be Kendal, for even its references to the castle and the games that used to be played there remain particularly vague and unsatisfying.

In contrast, the plot of ***The Disappearing Twins* (144)**, published in 1940, is a more fully realised story whose juvenile characters are drawn in greater depth. Most of the events take place in the usual generic Lake District setting of a large mansion house, Brandreth Hall, whose location is not revealed. However, towards the end of the story, Theodora Wilson Wilson moves the action to the well-known north Cumbrian seaside town of Silloth. There are detailed references to the sea front, 'a wide stretch of green', to its hotels and to a comfortable cottage from whose garden they 'could run straight down to the shore'.

While we are in the vicinity of Silloth there is now the opportunity to mention another lately discovered series book by the prolific Kathleen Fidler. This is ***The Brydons at Smugglers' Creek* (145)**, published in 1946. There seemed little connection with this title and the world around the Solway Firth that has been encountered in such books as *Master Deor's Apprentice* and *The Year the Raiders Came* (see Chapter II). Ration books, farm girls, harvest homes and a branch railway that has now totally disappeared produce a strong nostalgic element in what is after all a very routine 'kids outwit black-market crooks' adventure. Even that old standby, the rescue from the rising tide, takes us on to familiar ground, or should that be mud? The climax of the story carries the kidnapped children and their family into another two Cumbrian districts: the railway and police stations in Carlisle and the lonely roads up by Shap Fell.

More extraordinary is ***The Clue in the Castle* (146)**, publication date unknown, by Joyce Bevins Webb, which employs a strange mixture of real and fictional locations and the most remarkable plot development in what may be classified as largely a girls' school story. Like Angela Brazil, Joyce Bevins Webb decides to invent a coastline for Westmorland and invest it with all the usual adventure story dangers. The other aspect of the book has the heroine living in Grasmere, and a crucial accident involving two bishops on Helvellyn. The connection between young Nita and the oldest student in the school proves to be quite stunning, and it would be unfair to reveal it here.

Angela Bull, whose story of *Wayland's Keep* (4) we examined in Chapter I, proved also to have written *The Doll in the Wall* (147), published in 1978, for much younger readers. However, disappointingly, it is difficult to discover anything about what prove to be very generalised locations.

All the time new children's fiction set in this attractive area is arriving in the market place. It is unfair to the modern authors to give any more than a quick mention. You will find that long-running series like the Home Farm Twins are still constantly being added to, and I note also another Puppy Patrol story by Jenny Dale called *King of the Castle* (148), published in 1999, which is about a Great Dane who lives at a castle in Cumbria. I should also mention *Run, Dad, Run* (149) by Dulcibella Blackett, published in 2004. Another modern holiday story centring round a teenage girl is *French for Kissing* by Sophie Parker (150), published in 2005.

I must mention *The Great Harlequin Grim* (151), which is a 2006 book. It is by Gareth Thompson and is set in a community called Torbeck which seems to bear many strong resemblances to Coniston. Next, in late September of 2007, I was lucky enough to meet Patricia K Caldwell, who assured me that *A Last Year at Vivians* (152) (see Chapter II) had just been privately published. I look forward to reading it and its successors with pleasure—another sequel, *¡Viva Vivians!* (153), was published in 2008. *A Last Year at Vivians* starts on Carnforth Station, and includes a trip from Ambleside on a steamer and a visit to a hotel in Morecambe. *¡Viva Vivians!* has an outing to Beatrix Potter's house at Sawrey, a journey to Windermere and a walk to Orrest Head.

Chapter X ended with the rather sad story of the missing book. This postscript, however, concludes on a happier note, for two more books have just turned up. How did I ever miss them! They are books set in real places that anyone can go to, in order to relive one of the special experiences of *Another Country*. (See La'al Ratty in Chapter II.)

Small Railway Engines (154), published in 1967 by the Reverend W Awdry, and *Jock the New Engine* (155) by his son Christopher Awdry, published in 1990, are tales about the Arlesdale Railway which is visited by the Thin and Fat Clergymen of the famous little Thomas the Tank Engine books. The four steam engines of the Arlesdale Railway are based on the four primary steam engines of the Ravenglass and Eskdale Railway. In fact they are amongst the locomotives that make up the different versions of La'al Ratty which can still be seen today. The real-life engine River Irt becomes Bert in the story, River Esk is renamed Rex, River Mite becomes Mike and Northern Rock, Jock. (The Irt, Esk and Mite are three rivers which run into the estuary at Ravenglass from the foot of the Scafells, the highest mountains in England.) On certain open days a very special version of Thomas, complete with character face-plate, comes from another railway to take his share of the passenger loads.

And so the journey continues. Perhaps you know of other children's stories, old or new, which I have missed. If so, I would be delighted if you would contact me via the publishers of this book and pass on your information.

APPENDIX I

HOW TO FIND THE BOOKS—THE THRILL OF THE HUNT

LET me immediately confess that I don't own all of the books that I have written about in these pages. I don't see this as an admission of failure but a sign of success. The search for elusive books can become one of the happiest parts of the whole process for the dedicated book-hunter. Three memories stand out for me:

For five years I searched for a copy of *Lakeland Adventure* by Peter Lethbridge, before a children's bookseller, who I now hope has become a friend, let me borrow her copy. Similarly, nothing can equal the pleasure I got when, thanks to a kind lady in Long Island, New York, I held in my hands a copy of *The Gates of Bannerdale*. Finally, only the intervention of the Elsie J Oxenham Abbey society in Australia ensured that I had access to the extremely rare first books in the Damaris series.

I have been remarkably lucky. Through the online community and my participation in several discussion groups, I have made a whole host of new friends who were prepared to trust me with books that were often counted amongst their most precious possessions. In some ways, the search taught me just as much about the world of children's books and their readers as the experience of reading and writing about the stories or visiting the places and drawing the sketch maps.

Buying second-hand is largely a matter of luck, and it can happen to anyone that they find just the very book they most want, at a surprisingly reasonable price, if they keep looking. I collect books for the stories and the illustrations. Other people are also deeply concerned or even obsessive about first editions and mint condition. Certain children's books are not just a precious legacy from a talented writer, they are also a highly valuable and marketable commodity. Less often, a rare book may turn up reasonably priced. Below, I have listed various resources for tracking down the books you want. It is also always worth having a quick rummage at charity shops, charity stalls, jumble sales, car boot sales and the specialist Oxfam bookshops. You just never know what will turn up!

Online booksellers

Thousands of small second-hand booksellers now advertise their books online via a variety of websites. AbeBooks (www.abebooks.co.uk or www.abebooks.com if you are outside the UK) is currently the best known, but you could also try Biblion (www.biblion.co.uk or www.biblion.com) and Alibris (www.alibris.co.uk or www.alibris.com). Amazon (www.amazon.co.uk or www.amazon.com) has a large second-hand section, and www.bookfinder.com is a specialist search engine that searches through other sites. With these names, you can access sites that will enable you to scour millions of titles held by thousands of booksellers worldwide, with the possibility of homing in on a copy that you want. Don't forget to build into the money you are spending the cost of packing and postage, which will be quoted either by the selling organisation or by the individual bookseller.

AbeBooks and other online booksellers' lists cover the whole world, usually listing the home country's booksellers first. You may be surprised to discover that it is sometimes cheaper to buy a British children's book in the USA or in Australia than it is to buy from a British bookseller. Make sure you scroll down any online list and look at all the possibilities.

eBay

Plenty of period children's books are sold on www.ebay.co.uk (www.ebay.com), especially the more collectable or well-known authors such as Trease, Hill, Oxenham or Lloyd. For example, a quick check shows that today there are copies of *Under Black Banner* and *No Boats on Bannermere* listed for Geoffrey Trease, and all of Marjorie Lloyd's Fell Farm books are there. There are instructions online about how to buy, how to sell and how to pay for items that you have bought. It is possible to register books that are on your 'wants' list, if none is currently available, so that you can be informed by email if they come on the market.

Children's Book Dealers

Great Britain is generally well served by children's bookshops and book dealers, many of which operate a catalogue service, by post or email. They will usually post overseas. Most dealers will accept a wants list and contact you if anything comes up. The Girls Gone By website (address given in the New Editions section below) lists many dealers who specialise in period children's fiction.

Libraries and Inter-Library Loan

Some of the newer books in this collection were published during the last ten years. Your local library may have a copy on its shelves. Failing that, the inter-library loan service can sometimes supply a copy of even the rarest book. That's how I managed to read *Lanterns over the Lune*, *The Farm in Mallerstang* and *The Hunting of Wilberforce Pike*.

New Editions

Girls Gone By Publishers specialise in reprinting rare collectible children's books to make those much sought-after but hard-to-find titles available to a wider audience. The books are printed in a paperback format with the unabridged text and complete artwork of the original. Some of the more popular authors of the past are now being republished in small print runs. The Bannermere series by Geoffrey Trease, some books by Elsie J Oxenham and some of the Wells series by Lorna Hill have all been recently reissued. However, such is their popularity that you must place your order early to be sure of getting a copy. Ask to be put on their mailing list for future catalogues. Girls Gone By can be contacted at www.ggbp.co.uk or write for a catalogue to Clarissa Cridland or Ann Mackie Hunter at GGBP, 4 Rock Terrace, Coleford, Bath, Somerset BA3 5NF.

INDEX OF REAL AND FICTIONAL PLACES
Real places appear in plain type, fictional places in italics

INDEX OF AUTHORS, BOOKS AND ILLUSTRATORS

ACKNOWLEDGEMENTS

THE author and publisher would like to thank the following for their help with the material in this book:

Random House and the executors of the estate of Arthur Ransome for permission to use the line drawings from *Swallows and Amazons*, *Swallowdale*, *Winter Holiday*, *Pigeon Post* and *The Picts and the Martyrs*;

Penguin Books for permission to use the cover illustrations from *Fell Farm Holiday*, *Fell Farm for Christmas* and *Fell Farm Campers*;

Orion Books for permission to use the dustjacket illustrations from the Gollancz editions of *Smudge of the Fells*, *Woorroo*, and *The Dragon of the Hill* by Joyce Gard; and the same firm for the permission to use the dustjacket illustration of *The Hiding Place* by Winifred Mantle;

Lucy Firth of Geoffrey Higham Ltd for permission to use the detailed quotations from *The Gates of Bannerdale* and *Black Banner Players* and other stories by Geoffrey Trease;

William D Hunter (Bill) of Arnside for permission to use his photographs of Arnside and Morecambe Bay;

Peter Lewis of Walney Island, Cumbria, for permission to use the many splendid aerial photographs of Wast Water, Windermere, Coniston, Grasmere, Derwentwater, Tarn Howes, Helvellyn and Ullswater;

Richard A Copping of the Ravenglass and Eskdale Railway for the images of the railway taken by Ken Cservenka;

Hilary Boulton of the Friends of the Chalet School library for the opportunity to read the Patricia K Caldwell Vivians stories;

The members of the 'Girlsown' and the 'Collecting Books and Magazines' online discussion groups for their many helpful comments and patient answers to my questions;

Barbara Cooper and John Tipper in Australia for their help with finding the rare Elsie J Oxenham texts;

The staff of High Heaton Library and Newcastle Libraries for their help in obtaining texts via the Inter-Library Loan scheme;

Sally Dore, Donna Wenaus and my editor, Tig Thomas, for allowing me access to texts from their own private collections.

Every effort has been made to trace and credit the owners of copyright material, but the author and publishers regret if they have inadvertently failed to do so in some cases. They would be glad to hear of any cases where they have failed to give the correct acknowledgements.

Girls Gone By Publishers

Many of the authors mentioned in *Another Country* have been published
by Girls Gone By, as listed below:

Angela Brazil
A Fourth Form Friendship

Julia Cotter
Pony Thieves

Lorna Hill
Border Peel
The Vicarage Children

Out of print:
Back-Stage
Dress-Rehearsal
Marjorie and Co.
Northern Lights
Stolen Holiday
Swan Feather
The Secret
Vicki in Venice

Malcolm Saville
The Gay Dolphin Adventure
Lone Pine Five
The Secret of Grey Walls
Seven White Gates

Out of print:
Mystery at Witchend
Strangers at Witchend
Where's My Girl?

Elsie J Oxenham
Goblin Island
Jen of the Abbey School
The Abbey Girls Go Back to School
The Camp Mystery

Out of print:
Maidlin Bears the Torch
Margery Meets the Roses
Peggy and the Brotherhood
Rosamund's Castle
Rosamund's Tuck-Shop
The Abbey Girls
The Girls of the Abbey School

Non-Fiction Titles relating to Elsie J
Oxenham:
Island to Abbey
*The World of Elsie Jeanette Oxenham and
her Books* (out of print)

Geoffrey Trease
Black Banner Abroad
The Gates of Bannerdale

Out of print:
Black Banner Players
No Boats on Bannermere
Under Black Banner

Books in print as at 31/07/08.
See the website for a list of dealers who may still have stock of out-of-print books.

For details of availability and ordering go to www.ggbp.co.uk or write for a catalogue to
Clarissa Cridland or Ann Mackie-Hunter, GGBP,
4 Rock Terrace, Coleford, Bath, BA3 5NF, UK.